Oprah Winfrey

by Adam Woog

LUCENT BOOKS
A part of Gale, Cengage Learning

GALE
CENGAGE Learning

Detroit • New York • San Francisco • New Haven, Conn • Waterville, Maine • London

GALE
CENGAGE Learning™

Dedication: To my daughter, Leah, who at a young age figured out that only a few degrees separated herself and Oprah Winfrey—"and Oprah knows everybody in the world!"

© 2009 Gale, Cengage Learning

LIBRARY OF CONGRESS CATALOGING-IN-PUBLICATION DATA

Woog, Adam, 1953–
    Oprah Winfrey / by Adam Woog.
        p. cm. — (People in the news)
    Includes bibliographical references and index.
    ISBN 978-1-4205-0128-5 (hardcover)
    1. Winfrey, Oprah—Juvenile literature. 2. Television personalities—United States—Biography—Juvenile literature. 3. Actors—United States—Biography—Juvenile literature. I. Title.
    PN1992.4.W56W67 2009
    791.4502'8092—dc22
    [B]
                                                            2008042758

Lucent Books
27500 Drake Rd.
Farmington Hills, MI 48331

ISBN-13: 978-1-4205-0128-5
ISBN-10: 1-4205-0128-3

Printed in the United States of America
1 2 3 4 5 6 7 13 12 11 10 09

Contents

Fame and celebrity are alluring. People are drawn to those who walk in fame's spotlight, whether they are known for great accomplishments or for notorious deeds. The lives of the famous pique public interest and attract attention, perhaps because their experiences seem in some ways so different from, yet in other ways so similar to, our own.

Newspapers, magazines, and television regularly capitalize on this fascination with celebrity by running profiles of famous people. For example, television programs such as *Entertainment Tonight* devote all of their programming to stories about entertainment and entertainers. Magazines such as *People* fill their pages with stories of the private lives of famous people. Even newspapers, newsmagazines, and television news frequently delve into the lives of well-known personalities. Despite the number of articles and programs, few provide more than a superficial glimpse at their subjects.

Lucent's People in the News series offers young readers a deeper look into the lives of today's newsmakers, the influences that have shaped them, and the impact they have had in their fields of endeavor and on other people's lives. The subjects of the series hail from many disciplines and walks of life. They include authors, musicians, athletes, political leaders, entertainers, entrepreneurs, and others who have made a mark on modern life and who, in many cases, will continue to do so for years to come.

These biographies are more than factual chronicles. Each book emphasizes the contributions, accomplishments, or deeds that have brought fame or notoriety to the individual and shows how that person has influenced modern life. Authors portray their subjects in a realistic, unsentimental light. For example, Bill Gates—the cofounder and chief executive officer of the software giant Microsoft—has been instrumental in making personal computers the most vital tool of the modern age. Few dispute his business savvy, his perseverance, or his technical expertise, yet critics say he is ruthless in his dealings with competitors and driven more by his desire to maintain Microsoft's dominance in the computer industry than by an interest in furthering technology.

In these books, young readers will encounter inspiring stories about real people who achieved success despite enormous obstacles. Oprah Winfrey—the most powerful, most watched, and wealthiest woman on television today—spent the first six years of her life in the care of her grandparents while her unwed mother sought work and a better life elsewhere. Her adolescence was colored by promiscuity, pregnancy at age fourteen, rape, and sexual abuse.

Each author documents and supports his or her work with an array of primary and secondary source quotations taken from diaries, letters, speeches, and interviews. All quotes are footnoted to show readers exactly how and where biographers derive their information and provide guidance for further research. The quotations enliven the text by giving readers eyewitness views of the life and accomplishments of each person covered in the People in the News series.

In addition, each book in the series includes photographs, annotated bibliographies, timelines, and comprehensive indexes. For both the casual reader and the student researcher, the People in the News series offers insight into the lives of today's newsmakers—people who shape the way we live, work, and play in the modern age.

It's Oprah!

Not many people are so famous that they can be immediately identified by just one name. Oprah Winfrey is one of those people. Her tens of millions of worldwide fans know and love her simply as Oprah. Even people who are *not* fans know her just as Oprah. Everybody, it seems, knows Oprah.

As all these people know, Winfrey is a talk-show host. Her daily program, *The Oprah Winfrey Show,* is seen by nearly 50 million viewers in 117 countries around the world—from Afghanistan to Zambia, as Winfrey likes to say. It is the highest-rated, longest-running television talk show in history, and it has transformed the very nature of the talk-show genre.

But Oprah Winfrey is much more than simply a television host. She is also the first African American to own a film and television studio and only the third woman to do so. She is an influential book promoter. She is an Academy Award–nominated actress. And she is the driving force behind a vast media empire that includes print, online, film, radio, and television content.

She is also, not coincidentally, a billionaire. And she is one of the nation's top philanthropists, giving away a significant part of her vast fortune every year. In fact, Winfrey is the richest and most philanthropic black person of all time.

"God Had Another Vision for Me"

But this is not the end. Winfrey is far more than just another rich and famous media giant. She is also an inspiring role model for millions.

Oprah Winfrey was able to overcome the obstacles in her life to become a media giant.

Her enthusiasm for promoting social causes—and then for working hard to make them successes—sets an example for others. She urges her viewers to join in, thus raising millions more than what she herself donates. To use a phrase Winfrey might herself use: She walks the walk and talks the talk.

This role of guide seems to come to her naturally. Writer Marcia Z. Nelson comments, "Oprah Winfrey . . . is not ordained [as a minister]. She is neither preacher nor religious professional. Yet her multimedia empire . . . has given her the scope and stature of an influential leader."[1]

Winfrey has earned this power for many reasons. Perhaps chief among these is that her fans recognize her ability to overcome adversity in her own life. Winfrey has prevailed despite obstacles that might have crushed others.

Going with the River

Winfrey is deeply spiritual and has strong religious beliefs, which she often discusses on her show. To her, a strong spiritual basis is a necessary ingredient to leading a better life—a philosophy she tries hard to convey.

Although Winfrey has embraced many schools of spiritual thought, her own religious upbringing in the Southern Baptist tradition is still strong. Winfrey says she reads a Bible verse every morning and still prays on her knees, as her grandmother taught her.

But she also says that her life is directed by a kind of supernaturally inspired instinct, not connected necessarily with traditional religion. She comments, "I am guided by a higher calling. It's not so much a voice as it is a feeling. If it doesn't feel right to me, I don't do it. It is easier to go with the river than to try to swim upstream. Anything negative that happens to me is because I've been fighting against the stream."

Quoted in Richard Zoglin, "Lady with a Calling," *Time*, August 8, 1988. www.time.com/time/magazine/article/0,9171,968069,00.html.

These obstacles are numerous. She is an African American and a woman. She grew up in poverty and in a broken home. She experienced sexual abuse at an early age. Despite these factors, Winfrey has prevailed. And she did it almost completely on her own, though she is quick to also credit her deep religious faith for her success. She says, "The voices of the world told me I was poor, colored, and female. But God had another vision for me."[2]

Empathy

Winfrey's personal characteristics are, in large part, the reason so many people admire her. She is naturally strong, driven, and intelligent, and she is a charismatic, gifted speaker. British writer Paul Harris comments:

> Her riches and power seem almost a byproduct of her success at overcoming her past. "To have the kind of internal strength and internal courage it takes to say, 'No, I will not let you treat me this way', is what success is all about," she told an interviewer, dismissing the success of wealth in favour of simply surviving the abuse of others.[3]

Winfrey has used her natural characteristics to her advantage in creating her wildly successful television show. In particular, she has used them to perfect a highly personal, emotional, and confessional style of public conversation. As a result, no matter what the topic is, her show is always entertaining.

Winfrey's fans love how her strong empathy for others encourages guests to speak freely. People instinctively relate to her. Guests on her show seem to sense that Winfrey—unlike the average talk-show host—will listen carefully to them, be genuinely interested, and will genuinely care. And her fan base, which is about 75 percent women, picks up on that.

Candor

Another major part of Winfrey's appeal is her candor. Her willingness to be frank about her own shortcomings strikes a responsive chord with her audience.

Oprah's willingness to share the troubles and joys of her life is part of her appeal to her fans.

Winfrey is not always completely forthcoming. She kept certain parts of her past, and certain aspects of her family, secret for many years. Among these secrets was an early pregnancy that was revealed only when her half sister sold the story to a gossipy newspaper.

Mostly, though, Winfrey tells her audience everything, and they love her for it. Many observers feel that this is "a girl thing." Writer Deborah Tannen notes, "Girls' and women's friendships are often built on trading secrets. Winfrey's power is that she tells her own, divulging that she once [was such a compulsive eater that she] ate a package of hot-dog buns drenched in maple syrup, that she had smoked cocaine, even that she had been raped as a child."[4]

Not only is she very frank about her weaknesses and faults, but she is also very funny. Winfrey's wit is an important part of her appeal. Talking about her constant battle with her weight, for instance, she once joked, "I wake up in the morning, I go and look in the mirror sometimes, and one of the reasons why I realized I don't have a handgun is because I would have shot off my thighs years ago."[5]

Criticism

Everyone may know Winfrey, but not everyone loves her. Critics dismiss her television show as empty babble and disdain her charity as noisy self-advertisement. On a personal level, she has been accused of being overbearing and high-handed. And some people feel that she is sometimes guilty of spending her wealth in extravagant ways.

The content of Winfrey's show has been the target of particular criticism. When it started, *The Oprah Winfrey Show* specialized in sensationalistic, sometimes lurid topics. The success of this style led to a slew of Winfrey imitators, each louder and more explicit than the last.

But the tone and content of Winfrey's program have changed dramatically over the years. Much of what she now presents is what she calls "Change Your Life TV," exploring how her audience can become better people and create a better world. And her topics often concern important social issues, such as sexual abuse, drug addiction, or the rights of homosexuals. Nonetheless, Winfrey is still sometimes accused of playing a role in the "dumbing down" of television, the process of reducing programming to its lowest level.

Influence

Clearly, her fans disagree. And, thanks to this broad fan base, Winfrey remains a deeply influential part of today's society. This has been acknowledged in a number of ways.

Television network CNN has called her the world's most powerful woman. *Time* magazine listed her as one of the one hundred people who most influenced the twentieth century. *Life* magazine called Winfrey the most influential woman, and the most influential black person, of her generation. Furthermore, *Vanity Fair* magazine has suggested that she may have more influence on today's culture than any university president, politician, or religious leader, except perhaps the pope.

This influence is quick to show its power. If Winfrey endorses a book, it becomes an instant best seller; a negative comment about

Just Like an Ordinary Woman

A udiences love Oprah Winfrey, in large part because she seems so genuine. She has the ability to make her viewers feel like she is a personal friend. Of course, this is an illusion. As she often points out, she is no substitute for a real friend—for one thing, her viewers cannot call her up in the evening.

Nonetheless, they consistently relate what she says to their own concerns, problems, and interests. And they love Winfrey's informal, down-to-earth manner. (If her feet hurt, for instance, she is not afraid to kick off her shoes on camera.)

Women, who make up 75 percent of Winfrey's audience, seem especially open to her personal style, which often focuses on her own shortcomings (such as her famous struggle with weight). Sociologist Eva Illouz comments, "Oprah's persona seems to have emerged not in spite of but *precisely thanks* to her failures. . . . Oprah Winfrey casts herself as the condensed version of the problems that plague the most ordinary of women."

Quoted in Marcia Z. Nelson, *The Gospel According to Oprah.* Louisville, KY: Westminster John Knox, 2005, pp. 1–2.

a product can affect an entire trade. Paul Harris comments, "Only in America can a figure such as Oprah emerge to such dominance. Only in America can a woman who spends her days in an orgy of confessional, feel-good television become so powerful she can make or break careers [and] even threaten entire industries."[6]

Everybody may know Oprah Winfrey. Millions may love her and look up to her. Her early life, however, did not indicate that her future would be particularly bright.

Chapter 1

Starting Out

Orpah Gail Winfrey was born in Kosciusko, a small town in central Mississippi, on January 29, 1954. The baby's name, chosen by her great-aunt Ida, honored a figure in the Old Testament of the Bible.

Somewhere along the way, *Orpah* became *Oprah*. There are two versions of how this happened. According to one, no one could pronounce *Orpah,* and it became *Oprah*. Another version says that a nurse or midwife misspelled the name on the birth certificate. In either case, *Oprah* stuck.

A sign marks the site of Oprah's childhood home in Kosciusko, Mississippi.

FIRST HOME SITE OF
· Oprah Winfrey ·

KOSCIUSKO, MISSISSIPPI

On January 29, 1954, Oprah Winfrey was born in a wood frame house located on this site to Mr. and Mrs. Vernon Winfrey. She resided here as a child before moving to Milwaukee at age six. Within walking distance is the church where she made her first appearance in an Easter recitation.

She grew in the information/entertainment industry to become the world's foremost TV talk show host with a daily audience in the millions. At the same time she never forgot or overlooked her heritage and has been a regular supporter of folks back home as well as a role model to much of America.

Oprah Winfrey Was Born Here

K osciusko, Mississippi, is Winfrey's hometown. (Locals pronounce it Ka-zee-ESS-ko.) It is the seat of Attala County in a rural part of central Mississippi. About seven thousand people live there. It sits on the historic Natchez Trace Road, which in America's early days of settlement was an important road between Nashville, Tennessee, and Natchez, Mississippi. Kosciusko is named for a Polish general and engineer who helped America by serving on George Washington's staff during the Revolutionary War.

After she left as a young child, Winfrey never returned to live in Kosciusko. However, the town is proud of its famous daughter. Among other things, it has named a road in her honor. Oprah Winfrey Road, formerly Buffalo Road, passes by both the church she attended and her birthplace (a house that has since been torn down).

"Spectacularly Inauspicious"

Nothing about her birth indicated the baby's extraordinary future. In fact, writer Paul Harris asserts, "Oprah's birth was spectacularly inauspicious."[7] This was true for several reasons.

First of all, Oprah was African American. The lives of black people, especially those in the Deep South, would change dramatically as the civil rights movement took root in later years. In 1954, however, the prospects for African Americans in Mississippi were grim. For a female, they were especially bad.

Also, Oprah's parents were not married. They were not even a steady couple. And they were young: Oprah's mother, Vernita Lee, was eighteen when she gave birth. Her father, Vernon Winfrey, was a twenty-year-old military man at Camp Rucker, Alabama.

When Vernon finished his term of service, he moved to Nashville, Tennessee, and worked as a janitor and a dishwasher.

He apparently had not even known that Vernita Lee was pregnant. It appears that he learned about Oprah when he received a newspaper clipping announcing the birth. Attached was a note asking for clothes.

Earlist and Hattie Mae

For her first years, Oprah lived with her mother and grandparents, Hattie Mae and Earlist Lee, on their small farm. It was a modest place, without electricity or indoor plumbing and with only a few animals. Oprah's family was so poor that she wore overalls made from potato sacks.

When Oprah was a few years old, the cotton mills in town closed down. This meant that jobs were scarce. Vernita Lee heard she could find work cleaning houses in Milwaukee, Wisconsin. She moved there and left Oprah with Hattie Mae and Earlist.

There were few other children in Oprah's life and no close neighbors. Earlist, also called Earless, was little more than a distant, scary presence to young Oprah. She later recalled, "I feared him. . . . I remember him always throwing things at me or trying to shoo me away with his cane."[8]

So the strongest presence in Oprah's life was Hattie Mae. She was strict and not afraid to whip Oprah with a switch for misbehaving or avoiding chores. This punishment was so rough and so frequent that today it would be considered child abuse. In that time and place, however, it was simply the way things were done.

"The Preacher"

But Hattie Mae could also be supportive. Winfrey says that her grandmother taught her the importance of hard work, religious faith, and self-confidence: "I am what I am because of my grandmother; my strength, my sense of reasoning, everything. All of that was set by the time I was six years old. I basically am no different now from what I was when I was six."[9]

Another gift Hattie Mae gave young Oprah was an early ability to read. Books became her refuge from life's hardships and disappointments. They remained a lifelong source for learning, inspiration, and imagination.

Hattie Mae also recognized that Oprah was a champion talker. (The older woman once remarked that her granddaughter was onstage from the time she learned to talk.) Hattie Mae encouraged the girl to give readings and presentations at their church, Faith United Mississippi Baptist Church.

Oprah enjoyed the attention from these first speaking engagements. She says, "It was a way of getting love."[10] But there was a

"God Don't Mess with His Children"

Winfrey's grandmother, Hattie Mae Lee, took her regularly to her Baptist church and taught young Oprah lessons from the Bible. These lessons were not always straight, word for word from the Bible. They were Bible lessons as Lee interpreted them. Nonetheless, the girl learned them well. Winfrey recalls:

I remember when I was four, watching my grandma boil clothes in a huge iron pot. I was crying, and Grandma asked, "What's the matter with you, girl?" "Big Mammy," I sobbed, "I'm going to die someday." "Honey," she said, "God don't mess with his children. You gotta do a lot of work in your life and not be afraid. The strong have got to take care of the others."

I [later] came to realize that my grandmother was loosely translating from the epistle [to the] Romans in the New Testament—"We that are strong ought to bear the infirmities of the weak" (Romans 15:1). Despite my age, I somehow grasped the concept. I knew I was going to help people, that I had a higher calling, so to speak.

Quoted in LaTonya Taylor, "The Church of O," *Christianity Today*, April 1, 2002. www.christianitytoday.com/ct/article_print.html?id=8491.

Oprah's first experience with public speaking was at the church she attended with her grandparents in Kosciusko, Mississippi.

downside: Other kids cruelly nicknamed her "the Preacher." Still, it was worth it. Today, Winfrey calls her early experiences in church the "beginning of my broadcasting career. I loved being in front of people, dressed up, and being able to say my piece."[11]

Wisconsin

When Oprah was about four, Earlist died. Hattie Mae, a widow in poor health, found it increasingly difficult to raise Oprah. Vernita Lee returned and took her daughter to Milwaukee.

The cold northern city was a huge change from slow-paced southern farm life. Oprah's home now was in a cramped boardinghouse apartment with Lee and a second child—Oprah's half sister, Patricia.

Oprah felt like an outsider there. Lee was often gone—she worked long hours as a housemaid—and when she was home she was tired. Any attention she did have for her children was focused on little Patricia.

But there were bright spots in Milwaukee for Oprah. One was the realization that she was ahead of other kids. When she started kindergarten, she could already read. She wrote her teacher a note, politely pointing out that she did not belong there. The teacher agreed, and Oprah skipped a grade.

Nashville

Lee had trouble raising two kids by herself. When Oprah was eight, Lee contacted Vernon Winfrey in Nashville and asked him to take care of the girl for a while. Vernon, now married and working as a barber, agreed. He came for her in the summer of 1962.

Life in Nashville was another big adjustment. Vernon was essentially a stranger, and Oprah did not know his wife, Zelma, at all. But they were happy to have her as they had no children of their own. And their modest brick house was wonderful compared to the grim boardinghouse; for the first time, Oprah had a bedroom to herself.

Vernon and Zelma were supportive of Oprah, but they were also strict. They made her study hard, and they took her regularly to their church, the Progressive Missionary Baptist Church. She thrived in Nashville, skipping another grade, fourth, and further developing her reputation for public speaking.

A Grim Life

After Oprah spent a year in Nashville, Lee brought her back to Milwaukee. A third child, Jeffrey—Oprah's half brother—was now part of her family.

Vernon was not happy to see Oprah go. He worried that her life in Milwaukee was unhealthy. "We had brought her out of that atmosphere," he commented later. "I knew it was not good for her, being in that environment again."[12]

Why Lee wanted Oprah back is not clear since she continued to ignore the girl and pay attention to her younger siblings. Lee also ridiculed Oprah's love of books. Still, reading became Oprah's refuge from this unhappy life. She later remarked, "I don't know why my mother ever decided she wanted me. She wasn't equipped to take care of me. I was just an extra burden on her."[13]

This life was unhappy enough for the girl, but it got far worse. Beginning when she was nine, Oprah was sexually molested. The first to abuse her was a nineteen-year-old cousin. Afterward, he took the terrified girl out for ice cream and made her promise to keep it secret.

Later, two more men assaulted her: an uncle and a family friend. She was again forced to keep silent. They told her that the abuse happened because there was something wrong with her, and that she could never tell anyone.

Oprah, not knowing otherwise, believed them. She kept the secret for many years, and it powerfully affected her life. She says now, however, that there was a silver lining. After she finally made the abuse public, she became a tireless crusader to protect other children from similar damage. Perhaps, she says, others will be spared.

"I Can Do That"

Oprah's life had few bright spots during this period. One was the rare chance to see African American artists on television, such as the night Oprah saw beautiful and graceful black women on a top-rated variety program. "The first time I saw Diana Ross and the Supremes on *The Ed Sullivan Show*," she recalls, "it changed my life."[14] Another inspiration was Sidney Poitier, the first black man to win an Academy Award for Best Actor. Oprah says, "It was the first time I thought, 'I can do that.'"[15]

Her academic life, at Lincoln Middle School in Milwaukee's inner city, was also generally good. Oprah did not have many friends, but she got excellent grades. A concerned teacher, Eugene Abrams, enrolled her in a program to help gifted but underprivileged students. This helped Oprah earn a spot at a prestigious school, Nicolet High School in suburban Glendale.

Diana Ross (right) and the Supremes' appearance on The Ed Sullivan Show *in 1969 inspired Oprah to pursue her dreams.*

Academically, Nicolet was a step up, but it came at a price. To get there, Oprah had to take three buses each way. Many of her fellow passengers were African Americans like her mother, headed to menial jobs in the homes of white suburbanites.

Furthermore, Oprah was the only nonwhite student in a school of two thousand. She did make some friends, especially since by then the civil rights movement was flourishing. It was fashionable among liberal white students to have a black friend.

But being around these affluent students was often painful. Oprah recalls, "I was feeling a sense of anguish, because [the] life that I saw those children lead was so totally different from what I . . . saw when I took the bus home with the maids in the evening."[16]

In Trouble

As she grew into her teen years, the strong forces in Oprah's life came into opposition. She was smart and had a powerful will to succeed, but she was also battling neglect, poverty, and abuse. Not surprisingly, she started to rebel and act out.

On one occasion, she faked a robbery in her house because she wanted new glasses. She smashed the cheap, ugly ones her mother had bought and tried to make it seem that this had been part of the robbery.

More seriously, she briefly ran away from home and experimented with sex and drugs. In desperation, Oprah's mother took her for an interview to be committed to a home for wayward girls in 1968. Oprah recalls, "I remember going to the interview process, where they treat you like you're already a known convict, and thinking to myself: How in the world is this happening to me? I was fourteen, and I knew that I was a smart person. I knew I wasn't a bad person, and I remember thinking: How did this happen? How did I get here?"[17]

There was a waiting period before she could be put into the home. During this time, Lee contacted Vernon Winfrey, and he took Oprah back to Nashville.

But Oprah had a secret: She was pregnant. She kept her condition secret from Vernon and Zelma as long as she could. When she did give birth, to a son, he was premature and died after just a few weeks.

In Nashville

As before, Vernon and Zelma were strict but supportive with Oprah. They enacted a curfew, made her write a weekly book report, and had her memorize twenty new vocabulary words a week. Report cards with all A's and regular attendance at the Progressive Missionary Baptist Church were required. And she had to work part time in the grocery store Vernon had next to his barbershop.

Oprah hated selling popsicles and penny candy, but overall the discipline and structure of her new home worked. She stayed out of trouble, dressed demurely, and wore her hair in a conventional flip. She often went by her more common middle name, Gail. And she blossomed into an honors student at East Nashville High School.

Oprah has often credited Vernon, by all accounts a deeply responsible and moral man, for getting her back on track. In later years there has been speculation that he may not be her biological father. But she says it does not matter. He took her in and raised her, and she has always proudly called him her father.

There was another enormous influence on Oprah during this period. Maya Angelou's autobiography, *I Know Why the Caged Bird Sings,* is a beautifully written but unsparing account of the poet's struggles with poverty and sexual abuse. Winfrey says the book changed her life because Angelou's experiences were so close to her own: "I thought she was talking about my own life."[18]

"Grand Old Oprah"

Meanwhile, Oprah was developing her gift for oratory. She spoke publicly in a variety of settings. Often, her speeches were based on sermons. Deacon Carl Adams, a founding member of the Winfrey family's church, recalls, "She could just about hold you spellbound. She would always give something that was fulfilling spiritually."[19]

When she was sixteen, a pastor from Los Angeles heard her and asked her to come speak at his church. He paid her five hundred dollars—a huge sum of money for the young woman. On

Oprah Winfrey stands with her father, Vernon Winfrey, in 2003. She credits his strong moral presence with helping her get back on track after a troubled adolescence.

that trip, she saw Hollywood for the first time, and she swore it would not be her last trip there.

Oprah continued to excel at school. She was one of only two students from Tennessee selected to attend a national conference on youth. As a senior, she was voted "Most Popular Girl," and she dated the "Most Popular Boy," Anthony Otey. She joined the speech team and placed second in the nation in dramatic interpretation.

During her senior year she also was vice president of the student body. Her slogan was a pun on Nashville's famous country-music radio show, the Grand Ole Opry. She urged students to vote for "Grand Old Oprah."

Radio and College

During her senior year, Oprah visited a local radio station, WVOL. She hoped it would sponsor her in a March of Dimes charity walkathon. A disc jockey, John Heidelberg, liked her voice and suggested she audition. The result was a part-time job delivering the news—at one hundred dollars a week, more than her salary in Vernon's store.

Winfrey continued to work at WVOL after graduating and starting college in 1971. She had won a full scholarship to Tennessee State University. This prize came from an oratory contest sponsored by the Elks Club. Winfrey's speech, "The Negro, the Constitution, and the United States," was delivered in front of ten thousand people in Philadelphia, Pennsylvania.

In college, Winfrey studied speech and drama. She dated a boy named William "Bubba" Taylor. This appears to have been her first strong love affair. Winfrey also competed in several beauty contests.

In her first contest, she became the first African American to win Nashville's Miss Fire Prevention. The three finalists were asked what they would do with a million dollars. Two answered, sensibly, that they would donate it to family or charity. Winfrey just smiled and said, "I'd be a spending fool!"[20] Her unrehearsed candor delighted the judges and helped her win.

Oprah Winfrey (not pictured) competed in the Miss Black America pageant as Miss Black Tennessee, although she did not win.

On the Cusp of a Career

Winfrey went on to become Miss Black Tennessee. This made her eligible for the Miss Black America contest, although she did not win.

One thing that Winfrey was not during this period was political. She had no interest in black power, the social movement that swept the African American community during this time. Then and later, she frequently stated her belief that individuals—not ethnic, racial, or religious groups—are responsible for their own success or failure. She recalls, "I remember being, like, sixteen or seventeen years old, and I heard [the Reverend] Jesse Jackson at an assembly program say . . . that excellence is the best deterrent to racism or sexism. I sort of took that on as my motto. So whatever I did, I always wanted to try to be the best at it."[21]

Clearly, Oprah Winfrey was focused on finding excellence in her own career. That career was just about to start.

Chapter 2

On Television

Winfrey was offered her first television job in 1974, while she was still in college. WLAC-TV (now WTVF), the CBS station in Nashville, hired her as the station's weekend news anchor.

She was tempted. Winfrey did not like college and wanted to quit. She hesitated, however. She knew that her father would disapprove if she quit early. She also did not want to let down the Elks Club, which had given her a full scholarship.

What changed her mind was the advice of a professor she liked. He pointed out that one main purpose of college is to prepare students for a good job. Here was a good job, being offered by a prestigious television network! He encouraged her to take it.

She agreed and accepted the position. This made Winfrey the first female African American news anchor in Nashville—and, at nineteen, the youngest anchor ever. With her new salary, she made as much money as her father earned.

Winfrey did well in the job and was popular, but some black power advocates criticized her. They accused her of being a token—that is, someone who was hired only because she happened to be black, at a time when the station needed racial diversity. Her reaction was cheerful agreement: "Sure, I was a token. But honey, I was one happy token."[22]

Starting in Baltimore

Winfrey stayed at the station for about two years. She was then offered her first job outside Nashville. In this job, she coanchored

Oprah Winfrey's first job on television was as a weekend anchor on a CBS station in Nashville.

the six o'clock news at WJZ-TV, the ABC affiliate in Baltimore, Maryland. This was a much bigger market than Nashville, so it was a major step up.

She began her new job in the summer of 1976, but she was not a success. Winfrey's news-reading style was unorthodox. She usually did not read the news exactly as it had been written. Her style was slightly improvisational. Winfrey did not make up news,

The Battle of the Body Image

The station executives at Winfrey's first big job, in Baltimore, tried to remake her image. They sent her to a speech coach, which she found insulting—but which she allowed. Worse, they sent her to a fancy stylist in New York City for a makeover.

The stylist ruined her hair with a permanent that was too harsh. All of her hair fell out, except for a little bit in front. She could not find a wig that fit, so she wore scarves for months until it grew back.

The ongoing conflict between Winfrey and the station, and the humiliation of the botched makeover, caused tremendous stress for the young reporter. She found herself drawing on reserves of strength she did not know she had. She later joked that a person learns a lot about herself when she goes bald.

Winfrey began battling another problem during this period: her weight. She turned to food as a source of comfort from the pressures of her job. She lived in suburban Columbia, Maryland, across the street from a mall, and she would often walk there to gorge when she was stressed out or depressed. She recalls, "They had some of the best food stalls known to womankind."

Bob Greene and Oprah Winfrey, *Make the Connection: Ten Steps to a Better Body—and a Better Life.* New York: Hyperion, 1996, p. 3.

but she took the teleprompter writing as only a general guide, and she would use different words if they seemed more natural.

Her coanchor was an older man who was accustomed to reading exactly what he saw. He disliked Winfrey's style, and he disliked her personally. Nor were the executives at WJZ happy with her. Winfrey freely acknowledges now that she was out of her depth: "I was 22 years old. I had no business anchoring the news in a major market."[23]

"How Do You Not Cry About That?"

The station executives did not want to fire her, so they tried something else. They switched her to reporting. But this was even worse. Winfrey was naturally emotional, and she could not rein in her tendency to get caught up in stories. The cool, detached air of the typical news reporter was not for her.

This reached a crisis point when Winfrey's bosses forced her to interview a mother who had just lost her children in a house fire. Winfrey did not want to do it. She felt it was wrong to intrude on personal grief in that way. But they refused to back down, and because she wanted to keep her job, she went along.

Winfrey did the interview, but she also apologized on air to the grieving woman and the audience. She says, "It was very hard for me to all of a sudden become 'Ms. Broadcast Journalist' and not feel things. How do you not worry about a woman who has lost all seven children and everything she's owned in a fire? How do you not cry about that?"[24]

"It's Like Breathing"

Winfrey's fortunes changed dramatically when a new station manager arrived at WJZ. He wanted to start a morning talk show. He understood that Winfrey's emotional, improvisational on-air persona could be an asset, not a liability, in that atmosphere, and he tapped her for the job.

The new show, *People Are Talking*, was a local version of successful national programs like *The Today Show*. Winfrey's cohost was the affable, gray-haired Richard Sher. The show's debut in

August 1978 was promising, although Winfrey was still a long way from hosting celebrity superstars. The first guests on *People Are Talking* were an ice cream manufacturer and an actor from a daytime soap opera.

Nonetheless, the show was a hit, largely because of Winfrey. Television interviewers at the time typically did not react strongly to their guests' comments; they were busy thinking about the next question. But Winfrey was always present, paying close attention and connecting, laughing, and even crying when appropriate.

It was a perfect fit. The talk-show format let Winfrey do what she did best: chat with a variety of people, about everything from cooking and clothes to intimate personal details. It was a style

Affairs of the Heart

Adjusting to her new job in Baltimore was difficult, but not completely awful. For example, Winfrey made two lifelong friends while at WJZ. One was Maria Shriver, who was then a news anchor (and who would later marry Arnold Schwarzenegger). The other was Gayle King, then a production assistant at the station. King and Winfrey have remained best friends ever since.

She also found comfort in a romantic relationship with another reporter, Lloyd Kramer. Kramer was kind to her, but their romance ended when Kramer moved away to take another job.

Less successful was a relationship with a married man who treated Winfrey badly. The affair depressed her so much that she briefly contemplated suicide, even writing a farewell note to her friend Gayle King. Winfrey has since dismissed this, however: "That suicide note has been much overplayed. I couldn't kill myself. I would be afraid the minute I did it, something really good would happen and I'd miss it."

Quoted in Bill Adler, *The Uncommon Wisdom of Oprah Winfrey.* Secaucus, NJ: Birch Lane, 1997, p. 42.

Oprah Winfrey's casual, improvisational style made her show a hit with audiences.

Oprah's Chicago talk show became so popular that it debuted to a nationwide audience in September 1986.

that came naturally to Winfrey, who recalls, "I said to myself, 'This is what I should be doing. It's like breathing.'"[25]

On to Chicago

The show was such a success that it was beating even Phil Donahue's show in the ratings. Donahue was a well-known talk-show host, seen nationally and based in Chicago, Illinois. He pioneered the "tabloid" style of program and had ruled the talk-show world for years.

Her success attracted attention from other stations. In 1983 she accepted a new job. It was a bold move—to Chicago, Donahue's home turf and the third-largest television market in the country. She was to be the solo host of a half-hour morning talk show, *AM Chicago,* on WLS-TV, the city's ABC affiliate.

Chicago, "the Windy City," is a huge metropolis and can be intimidating to first-time visitors, but Winfrey recalls that she liked it immediately: "My first day in Chicago . . . just walking down the street, it was like roots, like the motherland. I knew I belonged here."[26]

Winfrey began broadcasting on January 2, 1984. Once again, her intimate style made her a hit. Within months, the show rocketed from last place to the top talk show in Chicago. She was beating Donahue in his hometown! A year after it debuted, the program was renamed *The Oprah Winfrey Show* and expanded to an hour.

The Color Purple

Another milestone in Winfrey's rapid career rise came in 1985. She was given her first major acting job in a supporting role in Steven Spielberg's film *The Color Purple*.

The story, based on a prize-winning novel by Alice Walker, takes place in the Deep South in the early- to mid-1900s. A poor girl, Celie (played by Whoopi Goldberg), tolerates years of abuse by an older husband (played by Danny Glover) before finding independence and a fulfilling life. Winfrey had loved the novel, considered it uplifting and inspirational, and was thrilled to be involved.

She was cast as Sofia, Celie's strong-willed sister-in-law. Sofia has also suffered abuse from men, but unlike Celie, she refuses to tolerate it. Sofia's proud, no-nonsense attitude causes her to confront the town's racist mayor and his wife. This altercation results in a beating, jail time, and years of sorrow.

Several experienced performers, including Tina Turner, were considered for the role. But Winfrey came to Spielberg's attention through Quincy Jones, an outstanding composer and music producer who was also one of the movie's producers. While in Chicago, Jones had seen her on television and knew she could play Sofia.

During the two months it took to shoot Winfrey's scenes, guest hosts and reruns filled the gap in her daily show. There was one unexpected aspect to the process. Winfrey had recently dieted

Oprah Winfrey's first major acting job was as the strong-willed character Sofia in the 1986 movie **The Color Purple.**

and lost some weight, but the film producers asked her to stop. They *wanted* her to be heavy.

"A Victory for All of Us"

Having never acted in a film, Winfrey was nervous. She was doubly so in the presence of Hollywood stars like Glover and Spielberg. On one occasion, she was unable to cry on cue. Spielberg assured her that it was fine, that they would shoot another day. Winfrey went back to her trailer and cried all afternoon because she had not been able to cry on demand for Steven Spielberg.

But Winfrey was eventually at ease with the process, and she delivered a solid performance. In fact, her character became more important in the film than originally planned.

For example, in one scene she was supposed to deliver a single line, but she improvised a long speech—and that speech became key to the film. While performing it, Winfrey drew on the example of Fannie Lou Hamer, a major figure in the civil rights movement who, like Sofia, stood up to repeated beatings and jail time. Winfrey recalls,

> I remember having sat there for three days of shooting, rocking at the table. Mine was the last angle to be shot. I had been sitting there watching everybody else. I had a lot of time to think about the years Sofia spent in jail, and the thousands of women and men, all the people who marched in Selma [Alabama, during the civil rights movement] who were thrown in jail, and what those years must have been like. Sofia finally speaking was a victory for all of us, and for me.[27]

At the Oscars with Stedman

Before the film came out, Winfrey was a celebrity only in the Chicago area. But her strong performance in *The Color Purple* put her in the national spotlight. Her performance was so powerful, in fact, that she earned an Academy Award nomination for Best Supporting Actress.

Winfrey went to the Oscar ceremony that year in Los Angeles with a date. She had met Stedman Graham shortly after moving to Chicago. Born in New Jersey, he had played professional basketball in Europe and had a daughter, Wendy, from an early marriage. Having earned a master's degree in education, Graham at the time ran a corporate marketing and education firm. In 1985 he also founded a nonprofit organization, Athletes Against Drugs.

They knew each other casually for about a year before Graham asked Winfrey out. After that, the romance blossomed quickly. They have been more or less steady partners ever since. She says, "He's kind and supportive—and he's six foot six [1.8m, 15cm]!"[28]

To attend the Oscar show with Graham, Winfrey—although battling her weight, as she had for years—wore a dress so tight that she had to lie on the floor and ask others to help to get it on. After the ceremony, she joked that she was thrilled to lose (to Anjelica Huston, who won for *Prizzi's Honor*). Winfrey had been afraid that climbing the steps to get onstage would have made her burst the seams.

Going National

Back in Chicago, the show was skyrocketing. The time was right to take it a step further and syndicate it nationally. This meant taping

Oprah Winfrey took a date to the Academy Awards in 1986, her boyfriend Stedman Graham.

the program, not broadcasting it live, so that it could be broadcast later all over the country by the stations that chose to buy it.

Winfrey was uncertain about signing a syndication deal. What helped persuade her was a discussion with her friend Roger Ebert, a Chicago-based film critic who had a popular syndicated television show and newspaper column. He predicted that in syndication, Winfrey's show would generate forty times the revenue of his own *At the Movies*.

Ebert was right. Starting with the first syndicated episode, on September 8, 1986, the show took off. It was soon the number-one daytime talk show in America, attracting double the audience of *Donahue*.

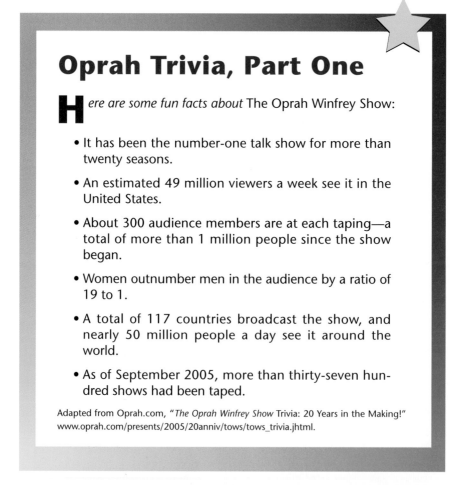

Oprah Trivia, Part One

Here are some fun facts about The Oprah Winfrey Show:

- It has been the number-one talk show for more than twenty seasons.

- An estimated 49 million viewers a week see it in the United States.

- About 300 audience members are at each taping—a total of more than 1 million people since the show began.

- Women outnumber men in the audience by a ratio of 19 to 1.

- A total of 117 countries broadcast the show, and nearly 50 million people a day see it around the world.

- As of September 2005, more than thirty-seven hundred shows had been taped.

Adapted from Oprah.com, "*The Oprah Winfrey Show* Trivia: 20 Years in the Making!" www.oprah.com/presents/2005/20anniv/tows/tows_trivia.jhtml.

*Harpo Studios is Oprah Winfrey's production company.
Owning this company made her the first black person, and
only the third woman, to have a major television/movie studio.*

Thanks to syndication, the money started adding up. At the age of thirty-two, Winfrey became not only the first African American television host to be nationally syndicated, but she also became a millionaire. For the next season, 1987–1988, Winfrey's income jumped to $30 million.

Harpo

When it had started, the show's production values were modest. Only a few people were needed. Sometimes they would find audience members by going out on the street, offering coffee and doughnuts. Winfrey did not even have her own office.

But that changed dramatically with syndication. More people and more sophisticated technology were needed. In 1988 Winfrey bought a dilapidated building in Chicago and created her own studio. The building had a colorful history. At the start of the twentieth century, it had been a military armory. In later years it was a roller rink and a television/movie studio called the Fred Niles Studio.

In its new incarnation, the building became Harpo Studios (her name spelled backward). Owning it made Winfrey the first black person, and only the third woman, to have a major television/movie studio. Winfrey was on her way to worldwide fame and fortune—and to changing the shape of television as well.

Chapter 3

Oprah Evolves

T he *Oprah Winfrey Show*—*Oprah* for short—has grown in popularity and scope since those first years. It also evolved. The biggest change concerned a basic shift in style and content.

In the early years, the show leaned heavily on sensationalist, "hot button" topics. For example, Winfrey once interviewed women who had children with their fathers. Other topics from this era included parents whose children had been injured by babysitters and women who gave up heterosexual relationships to become lesbians.

Critics condemned such shows as mindless and sleazy. But they were wildly popular with viewers, so Winfrey kept airing them. In 1987 a writer for *McCall's* magazine commented, "What *The Oprah Winfrey Show* does best is 'get-'em-in-the-gut' show topics. . . . Nothing is taboo."[29]

Talk Show or Therapy Session?

Winfrey was not the only television host, or even the first, to go into territory that is commonly called "trash television" or "tabloid television." Before Winfrey began her run, Phil Donahue was the genre's best-known practitioner. He was a tough interviewer who liked controversial subjects, and he encouraged confrontations among his guests.

In later years this style would be widely copied. Television hosts such as Jenny Jones and Jerry Springer would take trash television to new extremes. In the late 1980s, however, as *Oprah* ascended in the ratings, Winfrey outpaced the pioneering Donahue. Her enthusiasm and intimate, empathetic style hit a nerve with the audience. *Time* magazine writer Richard Zoglin noted in 1988:

> As interviewers go, she is no match for, say, Phil Donahue. . . . [But] what she lacks in journalistic toughness, she makes up for in plainspoken curiosity, robust humor and, above all, empathy. Guests with sad stories to tell are apt to rouse a tear in Oprah's eye. . . . They, in turn, often find themselves revealing things they would not imagine telling anyone, much less a national TV audience. It is the talk show as a group therapy session.[30]

Phil Donahue interviews guests on the set of **The Phil Donahue Show.** *Oprah Winfrey patterned the early years of her show on Donahue's brand of "trash television."*

Spirits and Sass

Winfrey developed her lively, self-assured public personality early in her career. This excerpt is from an article by Richard Zoglin that appeared in Time magazine in the summer of 1988, some four years into her Chicago-based program:

> Her growing celebrity, not to mention the high-style hairdos and drop-dead outfits, often seems gratingly at odds with her down-to-earth TV image. And, there are Chicagoans who say that Oprah has forgotten her roots, that success has gone to her head.
>
> But she seems pleasantly unaffected by fame. Her conversation is a mix of calm self-assurance (one rarely hears an "uh" in Oprah's speech), erupting high spirits and down-home sass. She talks amiably to the fans who constantly recognize her on the street, and personally says goodbye to each member of the studio audience filing out of her daily tapings.

Quoted in Richard Zoglin, "Lady with a Calling," *Time*, August 8, 1988. www.time.com/time/magazine/article/0,9171,968069,00.html.

Leaving the Sleaze to Others

Over time, however, Winfrey changed direction. She grew tired of trash television and began moving away from lurid, shocking topics. Winfrey says that she wanted instead to discuss social and spiritual issues that would positively affect the lives of her viewers.

The turning point, she says, came in 1989. She had as her guests a trio of people—a husband, his wife, and his girlfriend. Unexpectedly, the husband made a surprise announcement: His girlfriend was pregnant.

Winfrey commented later that she was shocked by the pained expression on the wife's face. The television host told the woman how sorry she was that she (the wife) had to hear that news for the first time in front of a television audience. It was at that point, Winfrey says, that she knew she needed to change.

It was gradual. Winfrey still relied sometimes on shocking subjects. By the mid-1990s, however, the show was dramatically different. By 1998 it was focusing almost completely on what Winfrey calls "Change Your Life TV."

Winfrey was especially focused on topics that were of particular interest to women since they were her core audience (as they still are). For example, among the topics the show covered were heart disease, abuse by spouses, and ways to meditate.

The change in direction was meant to educate as well as entertain viewers. Winfrey personally set the tone, demonstrating that she herself was trying to be a better, happier person—and that others could too. Writer Cecilia Konchar Farr comments, "Leaving sleaze to Jerry Springer, Winfrey moved on and began using her daytime talk show overtly [openly] to educate American women."[31]

Personally Important Topics

It was natural that Winfrey would choose topics that would attract viewers. But it also made sense that she would choose topics of particular concern to herself. These topics reflected—and still reflect—her own characteristics.

For example, Winfrey is socially and politically liberal. She is black. She is a woman. She is a devoted reader. She spends much of her time in great urban centers. She loves to eat. In her past, she has experienced poverty, abuse, and destructive relationships. These aspects of her personal life are often reflected in the topics she presents.

One example is child molestation. Winfrey started "Oprah's Child Predator Watch List," which operates through her show and Web site. It is designed to help track down accused child molesters by offering rewards for them. The watch list was immediately successful. Within the first forty-eight hours of its existence, two of the men named on it were captured.

Another example of a recurring topic of personal importance has been the issue of tolerance. Her shows have regularly stressed the importance of tolerance of sexual and racial minorities. She frequently urges her fans to understand and accept unusual or different people and cultures.

Goose-Bump Shows

To this end, Winfrey has devoted many episodes to the problems of gay men and women. On one show, for example, Winfrey traveled to a West Virginia town where a gay resident who was HIV-

Convicted rapist Ernest Thomas Jr. is led out of the Lebanon County Courthouse in Lebanon, Pennsylvania. The fugitive was captured two weeks after Oprah Winfrey posted a $100,000 reward for his capture on her Child Predator Watch List.

positive had become a social outcast. This man had deeply divided the town.

Winfrey interviewed him and others, including the town's mayor (who had fearfully ordered the draining of a public swimming pool the man had used). Unlike a reporter, Winfrey made no attempt to remain objective. On air, she scolded the town's hostile residents for their lack of empathy and understanding.

Such shows have allowed Winfrey to provide extensive media coverage for minorities. Many observers say that minorities are more socially acceptable in this country because of her. They point out that when a minority is spotlighted in millions of living rooms via television daily, the chances for understanding rise dramatically.

Winfrey is thrilled to spotlight issues that are close to her heart. Asked by a reporter about her favorite topics, Winfrey replied, "The ones that have mattered the most have been when I've been able to change the way people think for the better. . . . [The episode] 'How to Protect Your Kids from Strangers' was a goosebump show for me 'cause I knew we were saving kids."[32]

Heavy Topics

Although she has for years stressed serious topics, Winfrey also remains committed to simple entertainment. These two concerns do not necessarily mix well. One way she can combine them is to ask celebrities on her show to talk about their own experiences.

In that way, viewers have the pleasure of seeing famous celebrities and, at the same time, learn something important. For example, actress Brooke Shields spoke about her struggle with postpartum depression after giving birth. On another occasion, athlete Lance Armstrong discussed his fight against cancer.

Winfrey balances appearances by famous people with visits from experts in particular fields. For example, a psychotherapist, Jill Murray, is a frequent guest and offers such advice as the warning signs of dating abuse among teenagers.

And the show often showcases ordinary people. One was Sandra Moss, who was featured in an episode about depression. Moss

Oprah Winfrey tries to balance coverage of celebrities with educational opportunities, such as when seven-time Tour de France winner Lance Armstrong came on the show with then-girlfriend Sheryl Crow to discuss his battle with cancer.

described her years of mental agony, even considering suicide, before she found the correct medication. She urged Winfrey's viewers to seek help if needed and said, "People don't have to get as ill as I got before I got help."[33]

Another "ordinary" guest was a viewer who had been inspired by one of Winfrey's programs. After seeing an episode on youth at risk, this person made a commitment to care for a troubled child. Winfrey commented that examples like that one summarized her hopes for the show: "I love TV! I love that television can do that. I love television that can make a connection like that."[34]

Talking with Celebrities

Of course, not all of the topics on *Oprah* are so serious. Winfrey likes to have fun, and she enjoys luxury, and many times her shows are devoted to fun and the good life. So she regularly presents segments on such topics as gift giving, cooking, and home decorating.

Often her shows highlight nothing more earthshaking than a gossipy chat with a famous person. One notable talk was an interview with singer Michael Jackson. Jackson is notoriously shy about interviews, but in 1993 he granted Winfrey a rare opportunity to visit his Neverland Ranch. The show was the fourth most-watched event in American television history, and the most-watched interview ever. It is estimated that 90 million people saw at least part of it.

In another celebrity interview in 2005, actor Tom Cruise unexpectedly went wild in the studio. He jumped up and down on a

Finally Meeting Paul

The thousands of interviews that Winfrey has conducted over the years have required skillful use of many qualities, including empathy, knowledge, and a playful sense of humor.

An example of the latter could be seen when she interviewed the legendary musician Paul McCartney. Her first question to him was, "Paul, when I was a kid growing up I had all the Beatles' posters on my wall. Every morning I'd go to the posters and I'd say, 'Dear God, please let me meet Paul one day.' I wanted to know: All that time, were you thinking about me too?"

Quoted in Bill Adler, *The Uncommon Wisdom of Oprah Winfrey.* Secaucus, NJ: Birch Lane, 1997, p. 120.

Oprah Winfrey's interview with Tom Cruise made headlines when he jumped on her sofa to express his excitement about his new love Katie Holmes.

couch like a kid, fell to one knee, and shouted—all to express excitement about his new girlfriend (now wife), actress Katie Holmes. The interview became instantly notorious and was widely parodied. Three years later, Winfrey visited Cruise's Colorado home for a quieter interview, during which she exclaimed, "This is so normal!"[35]

Interviews That Bombed

Winfrey has a gift for bringing out the best in interview subjects, even the biggest celebrities. Usually her shows work well, but things do not always go smoothly. Winfrey says that her worst interviewing experience was with movie icon Elizabeth Taylor. Taylor had asked Winfrey, before the interview began, not to ask about any of her marriages.

However, as Winfrey pointed out later, that was a difficult thing for someone like Taylor, a celebrity who has been married seven times, to request. Winfrey asked anyway, and Taylor's curt, uncomfortable replies created an awkward air. Winfrey tried to draw the movie star out, teasing her that she talked too much, but Taylor was not amused. The movie star later apologized and returned to the show in a better mood.

Sometimes a celebrity interview does not happen at all. In 2008 another film legend, Doris Day, turned down an opportunity to meet Winfrey. Even after Winfrey drove to the gate of Day's California house, the actress declined to meet with her.

And sometimes unsuccessful shows have not involved celebrities at all. In fact, there have been so many bombs that Winfrey and her producers once created a segment called "Our Most Forgettable Shows." It revisited some less-than-classic moments from the past, including a heated debate about the best way to unroll toilet paper. Winfrey jokes, "We weren't thinking about Change Your Life back then, just change your toilet paper."[36]

Private Life

Many fans and critics feel that the most successful episodes on *Oprah* are those that concern topics of personal interest to Winfrey. And, as a celebrity, her own life is of enduring interest to her fans. So it is perhaps only natural that elements of her private life have often become subjects on her show.

Her ongoing weight problem is perhaps the most famous and most discussed of these elements. Winfrey has for many years been candid about her struggles to keep her weight down and

Oprah Winfrey willingly shared her weight-loss struggles with her audience. In her highest-rated show, Oprah revealed her trimmer figure after losing sixty-seven pounds on a liquid diet.

about the various diets and exercise techniques she has tried. In fact, the show's highest-rated single episode was one involving weight loss. On this episode, Winfrey wheeled out a red wagon. It held 67 pounds (30kg) of animal fat, representing the weight she had lost on a recent diet.

Sometimes what viewers learn about Winfrey's personal life is heartbreaking. In 2004, for example, Winfrey revealed on air the existence of her half brother, Jeffrey. This had not been common knowledge before. She told her audience that he had been gay, and that he had died of AIDS. On another episode, she also revealed that she had used drugs when she was younger.

A Secret Revealed

Such admissions have been deliberate. Winfrey considered them carefully before making them public. At other times, however, Winfrey's personal on-air confessions have been impulsive and unexpected. Probably the most dramatic of these came while speaking with a woman who had serious mental health problems.

The woman reported that she had been sexually abused, beginning at the age of two. Winfrey recalled that, as the woman spoke, "The phones lit up with calls from women all over the country saying the same thing had happened to them as girls. The guest I was interviewing started crying, and I started crying and told for the first time that it had happened to me too."[37]

As Winfrey sobbed, she spontaneously talked about her own childhood molestation. She told her audience that she had never discussed it before with anyone because she was too afraid and ashamed. The television host's shocking, spontaneous confession made international news—and her bravery in making it public further endeared her to her fans.

Spirituality, Boyfriend, Dogs

Winfrey prevailed over abuse and other problems, in part, because of her own strong faith. Her show has often spotlighted this personal, deeply felt interest in spirituality and personal growth.

Oprah Winfrey and boyfriend Stedman Graham walk their dogs in a Chicago park. Both Graham and her dogs have been topics of discussion on her show.

Many aspects of religion and spirituality have helped Winfrey shape her set of beliefs, and she is open to a variety of viewpoints. Nonetheless, Winfrey retains, at her core, the Baptist faith with which she was raised. Writer Marcia Z. Nelson notes, "If Oprah's spirituality is a . . . picking-and-choosing [of] what works from the world's religions, its roots are deep in African American Christianity."[38]

Oprah Trivia, Part Two

More fun facts:

- The title of the first syndicated show was "How to Marry the Man or Woman of Your Choice."

- The single most-often-talked-about subject has been "Parenting and Family Relationships."

- More than 856 celebrities have been guests on *The Oprah Winfrey Show*.

- Julia Roberts is currently the most frequent female celebrity guest on the show. The late Luther Vandross was on eleven times, making him the most frequent male celebrity guest so far.

- Winfrey says that Adam Sandler was one of her most surprising guests. She thought he would be just a jokester, but he was charming, shy, and thoughtful.

Adapted from Oprah.com, "*The Oprah Winfrey Show* Trivia: 20 Years in the Making!" www.oprah.com/presents/2005/20anniv/tows/tows_trivia.jhtml.

Spirituality and serious issues such as abuse are regular topics for her show. But they are not the only parts of Winfrey's life that provide fodder for it. Often, the subject at hand is less dramatic or serious.

One enduring topic of discussion has been her partnership with Stedman Graham. (They were engaged in 1992 but have not yet married.) And several shows have been devoted to Winfrey's beloved dogs.

The need to come up with these and other topics for a daily show is powerful. Producing an hour-long program—every day, year after year, and decade after decade—is immensely difficult. Keeping things interesting and fresh has been especially crucial as Winfrey's media empire continues to grow.

Chapter 4

Expanding the Oprah Empire

A s her show has grown in popularity and scope, so has the number of projects that Winfrey and her Harpo Productions undertake. Owning her show in syndication gave her control over it. This, in turn, gave her freedom to control her time and schedule. For instance, taping shows, instead of always broadcasting them live, gives her greater flexibility.

She also has more freedom to choose future projects. As a result, Winfrey has been able to try her hand in many different areas. The "Oprah Empire" has thus expanded to include film, television, radio, the Internet, musicals, and print media.

Some projects have given Winfrey more chances to act, something she had wanted to do since she was little. For a long time her only opportunity had come during her days in Baltimore: a cameo on the soap opera *All My Children*. Its creator was a guest on Winfrey's show, which led to Winfrey's appearance on the soap opera—as herself, wearing the tidy Afro hairdo she then favored.

Winfrey's later success in *The Color Purple* had made her eager to do more acting. For example, she had a supporting role in a 1986 film adaptation of *Native Son*, Richard Wright's classic novel about a young black man in Depression-era Chicago. Winfrey's character was the young man's weary and beaten-down mother, and she joked that she was so busy and overworked that the role was not difficult to play: "Tired, honey. . . . I didn't have to stretch to play that character."[39]

Beloved

Native Son was not a success, but Winfrey loved acting and felt she would be good at it. In fact, she once joked that her skills at mimicking people are so great that she had to avoid watching Phil Donohue's show—she was afraid she would start to look like him. (He is a white male with a thick head of white hair.) On a more serious note, she says, "I'm a good interviewer largely because I taught myself how. But I was born to act."[40]

Winfrey had another chance to act in 1998, when she produced and starred in a feature film adaptation of *Beloved*. This novel by author Toni Morrison won the Pulitzer Prize in 1987. It tells the powerful story of Sethe, a former slave in the years after the Civil War.

Sethe's story affected Winfrey powerfully, and she was honored to be able to make a movie of it. She wrote a book about the experience, *Journey to Beloved*. It includes excerpts from a journal

Oprah Winfrey got a chance to act in another major motion picture when she made the movie Beloved *in 1998. While critically successful, the movie was a financial failure.*

she kept during the process, stunning black-and-white photos, and an essay by the movie's director, Jonathan Demme.

The film version of *Beloved* benefited from massive publicity, including two episodes of Winfrey's show that were dedicated solely to the film. It also got respectable critical reviews. However, audiences did not flock to it, and financially it was a failure. It lost an estimated $30 million.

More recently, Winfrey has provided voice-overs in two animated films, in each case playing the role of an animal. She was the voice of Gussie the Goose in *Charlotte's Web* (2006) and of Judge Bumbleden in *Bee Movie* (2007).

More Productions

Through Harpo Productions, Winfrey has been extensively involved in producing shows for television beyond *The Oprah Winfrey Show* itself. One of the first of these, which aired in 1989, was *The Women of Brewster Place*. This was a made-for-television miniseries based on a novel by Gloria Naylor. In addition to producing it, Winfrey also played one of the seven women in the story whose lives intertwine in dramatic ways.

The Women of Brewster Place was not a success with audiences, and critics generally found it dull. Nonetheless, the next year an ongoing series, *Brewster Place*, was based on it. The series did even more poorly in the ratings than the miniseries. Its run ended after only a handful of episodes.

Another Winfrey production, in 2005, was more successful: a made-for-television movie, *Their Eyes Were Watching God*. It was based on a 1937 novel by the distinguished African American author Zora Neale Hurston about a black woman in Florida in the 1930s and her voyage of self-discovery. The movie starred Halle Berry and was adapted by a well-known playwright, Suzan-Lori Parks. It was popular, received good critical reviews, and was nominated for several awards.

More recently, Winfrey has produced several other projects. Among them were two 2007 releases: *The Great Debaters* (a feature film starring and directed by Denzel Washington) and *For One More Day* (made for television and based on a novel by Mitch Albom).

More Television

Not all of Winfrey's work has seen the light of day. For example, Harpo shot a pilot for a situation comedy based on Winfrey's life and work, in which she would have played herself. But the pilot disappointed her, and it never went into production.

Mostly, however, she has supported winning projects. One prominent example is the *Dr. Phil* show. Winfrey first became acquainted with psychologist Phil McGraw when she was in Texas preparing for a lawsuit that had been filed against her. At the time he ran a company, Courtroom Sciences, that specialized in consulting for trial lawyers.

Winfrey hired the firm to help her analyze the jury, and she was impressed with McGraw's abilities to understand people's motivations. She later invited "Dr. Phil" on her show several times, where he was extremely popular. He became a weekly guest, and she helped him start his own very successful program in 2002.

Winfrey acted again in 1997 with a small but telling role on the television situation comedy *Ellen*. Winfrey played the therapist to whom the character of the show's star, Ellen DeGeneres, reveals that she is a lesbian. The real-life DeGeneres made this news about herself public at the same time.

Soon afterward, theater critic Mark Steyn used the show as an example of Winfrey's widespread influence. He pointed out that Winfrey's involvement in a project was now a genuine mark of value. Speaking satirically, Steyn wrote, "Today, no truly epochal [very important] moment in the history of the Republic occurs unless it is validated by [Winfrey's] presence. When Ellen said, 'Yep! I'm gay,' Oprah was by her side, guesting on the sitcom as (what else?) the star's therapist."[41]

Other Ventures

Moving beyond film and broadcast television, Winfrey has tried her hand in several other arenas. For example, she ventured into cable television by cofounding the Oxygen network. It is primarily devoted to women's issues and concerns. Oxygen debuted in 2000 and was bought by NBC in 2007.

Oprah Winfrey helped launch the career of the popular television psychologist Dr. Phil, shown here at the taping of his first show in 2002.

Winfrey was also in the restaurant business for several years. In 1989 she became a co-owner of an upscale Chicago restaurant, the Eccentric. The high-profile establishment featured Italian, French, and American cooking, with an emphasis on healthy recipes for dieters. However, it experienced several changes in chefs and poor sales, and it closed in 1995.

Winfrey's growing empire has also embraced the world of Broadway musicals. Late in 2005 she coproduced a musical version of *The Color Purple*. (One of the show's other producers was Quincy Jones, who had "discovered" Winfrey many years before for her role in the movie.)

This version of *The Color Purple* featured a number of theatrical heavyweights, including playwright Marsha Norman, director Gary Griffin, and songwriters Brenda Russell, Stephen Bray, and Allee Willis. *Oprah Winfrey Presents: The Color Purple*, as the

Winfrey and Rap

Winfrey has sometimes gotten into trouble with other celebrities over the years. For example, in 2006 several prominent rappers publicly criticized her. They accused the television host of having a bias against hip-hop music. One of them, Ludacris, said that Winfrey scolded him about his lyrics and edited out comments he made while on her show.

Winfrey responded by telling reporters that she liked some rap, but she opposed lyrics that put down women. She said she explained her position to Ludacris after his appearance. She also said she understood that his music was for entertainment purposes, but she worried that some of his listeners might take his words too literally and seriously.

musical was officially titled, had a successful run on Broadway before beginning a series of national tours.

In 2006 Winfrey moved into still another medium: radio. In an arrangement with XM Satellite Radio, she established a new twenty-four-hour channel, *Oprah & Friends*. It features many people familiar to regular viewers of *Oprah*, including Dr. Phil, Bob Greene (Winfrey's personal trainer), Gayle King, and Winfrey herself, offering a mix of talk, advice, and information.

Winfrey's expanding empire also includes an Internet presence. Her official Web site, Oprah.com, has up-to-date information, archived stories, and links to a wide variety of subjects. It has been extremely popular, averaging more than 70 million page views and more than 6 million users monthly.

In Print

Moreover, Winfrey has become a major presence in the publishing world. She is the name, face, and driving force behind one wildly successful magazine: *O, The Oprah Magazine*. She has also coauthored a number of books, all of them best sellers. They include *Make the Connection: Ten Steps to a Better Body—and a Better Life*, written with Bob Greene; and *In the Kitchen with Rosie: Oprah's Favorite Recipes*, for which she teamed up with her health-conscious chef, Rosie Daley.

Along with Winfrey's spectacular publishing successes have been occasional malfunctions. For example, Winfrey announced in 1993 that she had signed a deal to write her own story. She finished the eagerly awaited manuscript with help from coauthor Joan Barthel, then postponed its publication indefinitely.

O, The Oprah Magazine, launched in 2000, expanded Oprah's influence into the publishing world.

She felt that she did a good job of presenting the bare facts of her life. But Winfrey worried that the book would not be a therapeutic or healing experience for readers. She said she realized that she was not yet settled in her mind about some difficult subjects. Winfrey comments, "I was writing in the book about forgiveness, and . . . I thought, 'I'm not clear on the issue myself.'. . . I thought, 'Have I really forgiven? And is it right for me to put this in a book? And what influence will it have on other people?' I had no real clarity myself so I felt I had no business writing it."[42]

The Book Club Is Born

Despite her stalled autobiography, Winfrey has tremendous power in the book world. She can sell millions of books for authors simply by inviting them to appear on her show. Indeed, Winfrey's clout in the publishing world—called "the Oprah Effect"—is so great that her ability to sell books is estimated at twenty times

"Oprah's Roots"

For a program on public television in 2006, "Oprah's Roots" (part of the African American Lives series), Winfrey had her DNA tested. This genetic test provided a lot of information about her ethnic background. The test determined that her maternal (mother's) line comes from the Kpelle ethnic group, from the area that today is Liberia, Africa. Her genetic makeup is 89 percent sub-Saharan African. The test indicated that she is also part Native American (about 8 percent) and East Asian (about 3 percent).

The show revealed many other interesting details about her family roots. For example, her grandfather, Elmore Winfrey, was involved in the civil rights movement in Mississippi, housing and helping volunteers working on voter registration. Also, it was discovered that her distant cousin is the famed gospel singer Mavis Staples.

that of any other celebrity. D.T. Max, writing in the *New York Times*, calls Winfrey "the most successful pitch person in the history of publishing."[43]

The best example of this power is Oprah's Book Club. This regular feature on her show is modeled on the popularity of friends forming groups to discuss certain books. The idea came from one of Winfrey's producers, Alice McGee. The two often traded books and talked about them; then they realized they could expand the practice nationwide.

Winfrey understands that reading is essentially a solitary activity. But she also knows that it is a richer experience if the book is discussed with others. Cecilia Konchar Farr, a professor of English and women's studies, comments, "Oprah's Book Club is based on the same premise as Oprah's talk show—that novels, like sex, celebrities, and social problems, should be talked about."[44]

The Book Club Evolves

Oprah's Book Club was launched in 1996, and the results have been phenomenal. Since the club's debut in 1996, every book with an "O" on its cover, announcing that it is an Oprah pick, has sold more than a million copies. This began with Winfrey's very first choice: a novel by Jacquelyn Mitchard, *The Deep End of the Ocean*, about the terrible repercussions in a family after the kidnapping of a young child.

The club's choices have occasionally caused problems. One, picked late in 2001, was Jonathan Franzen's novel *The Corrections*. Franzen told reporters that he was somewhat dismayed at being chosen because he felt that many of Winfrey's previous picks were sentimental books with one-dimensional characters. An angry Winfrey promptly scratched Franzen from her list, but not before the media picked up on the story. Franzen tried to explain that he had not meant to be insulting, but the damage was done.

Soon afterward, Winfrey suspended the book club. She had always personally chosen each book, but now, she said, she could not maintain the pace. She could not read enough to find current books that were worth recommending every month.

Winfrey restarted the club in 2003, after a year off. For the new version, she decided to choose fewer books (three or four a year), with an emphasis on classics. Her first pick was Nobel Prize–winner John Steinbeck's *East of Eden*, a sprawling tale of two families in California's Salinas Valley first published in 1952. True to form, the book shot to the top of the best-seller list and stayed there—more than a half century after it first appeared.

"It's an Upheaval"

A few years after restarting the book club, Winfrey expanded it to include a wider range of titles and types, including nonfiction, current novels, and memoirs. One of these books caused another controversy. James Frey's memoir, *A Million Little Pieces,* was billed as an account of the author's life as an alcoholic, drug-addicted

Author James Frey got into trouble with Oprah when his memoir—promoted by her book club—turned out to be mostly fiction.

criminal. But critics revealed that the supposedly true account was largely fictional. At first Winfrey defended Frey, saying that his book had moved many people. But in a live televised discussion, Winfrey severely scolded Frey, and the author admitted that he had lied about many things. A number of critics applauded Winfrey's tough approach to making Frey take responsibility for bending the truth.

Oprah's Book Club continues to be influential, if only because of its success in promoting reading. Writer Paul Harris comments, "Oprah is single-handedly persuading millions of Americans to switch off their televisions and read a book (and talk about it afterwards). Government cannot do that; Oprah can."[45] And writer Toni Morrison commented on Winfrey's show in 1997, "When a beloved television personality persuades, convinces, cajoles hundreds of thousands of people to read books, it's not just a revolution, it's an upheaval."[46]

As elements of the Oprah Empire, such as her book club, have grown, so has Winfrey's financial gain. As her money has grown, she has remained committed to giving much of it away.

Chapter 5

Giving It Away

The expansion of Winfrey's empire stoked the furnace of her wealth to record-breaking levels. By the early 1990s, thanks to successful projects and shrewd investments, she was the richest woman in entertainment. By 1995 her net worth had reached $340 million. By 2007 it had ballooned to an estimated $2.5 billion.

All this money put Winfrey in rarified company. She joined actor-comedian Bill Cosby as the first two African Americans to make the "Forbes 400" list of the world's richest people. She also overtook Meg Whitman, the former chief executive officer of eBay, as the richest self-made woman in America. (*Self-made* refers to the fact that her wealth was earned, not inherited.) Furthermore, Winfrey became the nation's highest-paid television entertainer and the first black woman billionaire in history.

Her rise from poverty to extraordinary wealth has been the subject of much discussion and analysis over the years. It was even the focus of a college course that debuted in 2001. The course was titled "History 298: Oprah Winfrey, the Tycoon," and it was taught by Professor Juliet E.K. Walker of the University of Illinois.

Not Shy About Spending

Winfrey has never been shy about enjoying her wealth. She likes to buy things like expensive clothes and fine cars. She also owns a good deal of property. Winfrey's main residence these days is

"The Promised Land," a 42-acre (17ha) estate, complete with ocean and mountain views, in Montecito, California. Her show is still taped in Chicago, so she has a condominium there. And Winfrey has homes in Lavallette, New Jersey; Fisher Island, Florida; Telluride, Colorado; and Maui, Hawaii.

Winfrey says that she does not feel guilty about being wealthy when so many are poor. She commented in 2006, "I have lots of things, like all these Manolo Blahniks [shoes]. I have all that and I think it's great. I'm not one of those people like, 'Well, we must renounce ourselves.' No, I have a closet full of shoes and it's a good thing."[47]

Winfrey also likes to give gifts to those who are close to her. For example, she treats her staff well, rewarding them for their hard work. On one occasion, she paid for a wedding in Italy and honeymoon for one of her longtime producers. On another, in the summer of 2006, Winfrey celebrated her twentieth year on national television by taking her entire staff and their families to Hawaii—more than one thousand people in total.

Oprah Winfrey owns several homes, but her main residence is her 42-acre estate in Montecito, California.

And sometimes Winfrey gives away expensive items or experiences as part of a show. For example, a man who had gone from morbid obesity to a healthier size was featured in a segment on "Incredible Weight Losses." He told Winfrey on air that he had always wanted to sit in a Porsche. Minutes later he was presented with a new Porsche Boxster S, worth about sixty-three thousand dollars. On another occasion, she gave everyone in the studio audience a new car.

Philanthropy

But this form of giving things away is essentially a publicity stunt. Such stunts are meant to boost the show's ratings and do not necessarily involve Winfrey spending her personal fortune. A far more significant indication of her willingness to spend on others is her extensive philanthropy. Each year, Winfrey gives away tens of millions of dollars to worthy causes—and asks others to be generous as well.

Scholarships for Essays

Winfrey has sometimes combined her philanthropy with other aspects of her show. For example, in 2006 she selected Elie Wiesel's *Night* as one pick of Oprah's Book Club. *Night* is a memoir about Wiesel's time with his parents in Auschwitz, a German concentration camp, during World War II.

To augment the book club, Winfrey and Wiesel traveled together to Auschwitz. Then she held an essay contest in which fifty thousand high school students competed to be on a follow-up show. Fifty were selected. Many of the winning essays were by students who had endured discrimination and persecution of their own, such as homophobia and the Rwandan genocide. As a surprise to the winning students, AT&T gave each a five-thousand-dollar college scholarship. Winfrey personally matched this amount for a total of ten thousand dollars.

Winfrey recognizes that she has had extraordinary opportunities in her life. She gets tremendous pleasure from being able to give the same sorts of breaks to others—breaks in life that they might not otherwise have. She comments, "My mission is to use [my] position, power and money to create opportunities for other people."[48]

Winfrey's philanthropic activities have therefore been extensive. In fact, it is estimated that she donates more to charity than any other show-business celebrity in America. She has so far given away well over $300 million of her own fortune, with no signs of stopping.

This generosity has landed her on still another rarified list. In 2004 she became the first African American to have a place on *Business Week* magazine's annual list of the nation's fifty most generous philanthropists. As of 2006, she was ranked thirty-second on this list.

For Kids and Students

Winfrey's interests in philanthropy—in where her money goes—take several forms. Perhaps naturally because of the events of her life, these interests are generally focused on helping the disadvantaged and those who have had deprived or difficult childhoods. Winfrey has been especially interested in helping young people, people of color, and abused women.

For example, she has provided money to put hundreds of African Americans through college. She did this, in part, by establishing a series of scholarships in her father's name at the school she left, Tennessee State University in Nashville. (In 1987 she gave the commencement speech there and was given an honorary diploma.) She has also donated generously to such institutions as Morehouse College (a historically black school) and the United Negro College Fund.

Likewise, she has funded projects for young people that were not strictly academic. For example, she underwrote a Boys and Girls Club in her hometown of Kosciusko. Winfrey dedicated the 30,000-square-foot (2,787m²) building in 2006. In a statement about the project, Winfrey wrote, "I'm offering this center to Kosciusko as a place where children can dream big and know that with preparation and determination they can make those dreams real."[49]

Oprah Winfrey's philanthropy earned her the Elie Wiesel Humanitarian Award in 2007. Here she poses with Elie Wiesel at the dinner in her honor.

Oprah's Angel Network

Winfrey has also been tireless in inspiring other people to donate to worthy causes. To help this along, in 1997 she started Oprah's Angel Network. The Angel Network is designed to get people around the world to help improve the lives of the underprivileged. It began as an effort to collect enough spare change to fund 150 scholarships through the Boys and Girls Clubs of America and to volunteer time to build two hundred homes for the needy through Habitat for Humanity International.

"If You're in It to Make Money, Forget It"

In a keynote speech for the American Woman's Economic Development Corporation in 1989, Winfrey outlined her "Ten Commandments" for a successful life:

1. Don't live your life to please other people.

2. Don't depend on externals to help you get ahead.

3. Strive for the greatest possible harmony and compassion in your business and your life.

4. Get rid of all the back stabbers around you.

5. Be nice, not catty.

6. Get rid of your addictions.

7. Surround yourself with people who are as good [as] or better than you are.

8. If you're in it to make money, forget it.

9. Never give up your power to another person.

10. Don't give up.

Quoted in Bill Adler, *The Uncommon Wisdom of Oprah Winfrey.* Secaucus, NJ: Birch Lane, 1997, pp. 230–31.

The Angel Network has since grown wildly, thanks to Winfrey's ability to promote it. To date, the network has raised more than $80 million in donations. Winfrey covers all of the administrative costs for the network herself. That way, all of the donated money actually reaches those in need and is not spent elsewhere.

The network funnels money to many groups around the world. One project it sponsors is "O Ambassadors," a program that works with schools to inspire students to be active, well-informed citizens. Also, within a year it raised more than $11 million for relief after Hurricane Katrina devastated New Orleans and other parts of the Gulf Coast in 2005. Winfrey matched this by contributing $10 million of her own money.

"They Ask for Uniforms"

Winfrey frequently focuses her fund-raising overseas. For example, the Angel Network funds rural schools in twelve countries. Another example was "Oprah's Christmas Kindness," a 2004 program that focused attention on the plight of children in South Africa affected by poverty and AIDS. Winfrey and her crew distributed presents to fifty thousand children as well as backpacks full of school supplies, school uniforms, and other clothes.

Winfrey then used the show to ask her viewers to donate more money for the children. She promised that she would personally oversee where the money was spent. Winfrey's viewers around the world responded by donating more than $7 million.

South Africa has been the locale of an even bigger philanthropic project. Starting in 2002, Winfrey has invested more than $40 million in the ambitious Oprah Winfrey Leadership Academy for Girls. This school is located near Johannesburg, the largest city in South Africa.

It was inspired by a conversation between Winfrey and Nelson Mandela, South Africa's foremost champion of civil rights and its first democratically elected president. Mandela asked her to do something for the children of his country. She chose to build a school for academically gifted but impoverished young women in the hope that they would someday become their nation's leaders.

The Oprah Winfrey Leadership Academy for Girls in South Africa opened in 2007.

Some observers criticized Winfrey because she has not funded such an academy in America. Her response was to voice disappointment that so many young Americans do not value the opportunities they already have. She comments, "I became so frustrated with visiting inner-city schools that I just stopped going. The sense that you need to learn just isn't there. If you ask the kids what they want or need they will say an iPod or some sneakers. In South Africa, they don't ask for money or toys. They ask for uniforms so they can go to school."[50]

"A Place of Honor"

The academy began operation in January 2007. Its first two classes include 152 girls, age eleven and twelve, selected from among thirty-five hundred applicants. Eventually, the school will have hundreds of students from grades seven to twelve.

Its twenty-eight buildings are spread out on a large campus. They include comfortable dormitories, well-equipped classrooms, a beauty salon, and two theaters. Winfrey personally chose much of what the girls use, from china and bedsheets to uniforms and the beds themselves—she reportedly sprawled out on each bed to check it for comfort.

Winfrey also insisted that the dorm rooms and the closets be extra large, although the girls have only a few changes of clothes apiece. She explained the importance of this when she commented, "It's because they *will* have something. We plan to give them a chance to earn money to buy things. That's the only way to really teach them how to appreciate things."[51]

Some of the criticism about the school has centered on what is seen as extravagant spending for a small number of students in a vast and deeply impoverished nation. However, many people have defended Winfrey for providing opportunities for especially needy girls. Winfrey also says the expense is justified. She states, "These girls deserve to be surrounded by beauty, and beauty does inspire. I wanted this to be a place of honor for them because these girls have never been treated with kindness. They've never been told they are pretty or have wonderful dimples. I wanted to hear those things as a child."[52]

The Legends Weekend

Sometimes Winfrey focuses on honoring people in other ways besides money. A prominent example was the Legends Weekend, a three-day celebration she held in 2005. It honored twenty-five prominent African American women and was billed as "A Bridge

Oprah Winfrey threw the Legends Ball in 2005 to honor prominent African American women.

to Now—a Celebration for Remarkable Women During Remarkable Times."

Each of the honorees was a black woman who had made an outstanding contribution in the arts, entertainment, or politics. Winfrey commented about them, "These women, who have been meaningful to so many of us over the years, are legends who have been magnificent in their pioneering and advancing of African-American women. It is because of their steps that our journey has no boundaries."[53]

Among the honorees were two icons of the 1960s civil rights movement, Rosa Parks and Coretta Scott King. Others included singers Leontyne Price, Dionne Warwick, Patti LaBelle, Diana Ross, Tina Turner, Shirley Caesar, Gladys Knight, and Roberta Flack; activist Michelle Obama; actresses Ruby Dee, Cicely Tyson, and Diahann Carroll; and writers Terry McMillan, Alice Walker, Toni Morrison, and Maya Angelou.

"Squealing Like Seven-Year-Old Girls"

Also invited to the celebration were a number of what Winfrey called "the young'uns"—artists representing the next generations of black women. They included Alicia Keys, Ashanti, Angela Bassett, Kathleen Battle, Mary J. Blige, Brandy, Mariah Carey, Natalie Cole, Missy Elliott, Tyra Banks, Iman, Janet Jackson, Phylicia Rashad, Debbie Allen, Yolanda Adams, and Chaka Khan.

The three days of festivities took place mainly at Winfrey's California home. There were several events, including a lavish women-only luncheon. The lunch included, among other things, eighty cases of champagne from France, 120 pounds (54kg) of tuna from Japan, twenty thousand white peonies as part of the decorations, and entertainment by a symphony orchestra.

Each honoree had a personal waiter, and each of the more than sixty guests was presented with a red-alligator gift package holding engraved silver boxes and diamond earrings. Actress Alfre Woodard, commenting on the excitement this caused, told a reporter, "We were squealing like seven-year-old girls on Christmas Day."[54]

Other events included a formal evening ball attended by dozens of celebrities. Among them were Halle Berry, Spike Lee, Jesse Jackson, Tyler Perry, Sidney Poitier, Barbara Walters, Diane Sawyer, John Travolta, Tom Cruise, Quincy Jones, Smokey Robinson, and Barack and Michelle Obama. Eleven million people later saw a one-hour television special about the weekend.

Oprah's Law

Not all of Winfrey's formidable energy is devoted to philanthropic activities, honoring African American achievement, or even buying expensive shoes. As her popularity, wealth, and influence have grown, she has begun to flex her political muscles as well.

Often this activity has been behind the scenes. But one very public political fight started in 1991, when Winfrey became the driving force behind a national campaign to battle child abuse. She worked hard for passage of the National Child Protection Act. This federal law was designed to create a data bank of information about convicted child abusers. It was for use by schools and child-care agencies to ensure that dangerous people could not be hired in those places.

The first time it went to Congress the bill did not generate enough support. Then Winfrey produced and hosted an hour-long documentary on child abuse, *Scared Silent*. The program ran simultaneously on three national networks—a first for a program that was not a breaking (immediate) news story. *Scared Silent* was seen by 45 million people and generated more than one hundred thousand responses to an abuse hotline.

It also revived interest in passage of the data-bank bill. Support for what became known as Oprah's Bill grew, and the legislation passed in 1993. President Bill Clinton signed it into law. In his remarks to the public, Clinton singled out Winfrey for special praise:

> I thank you, Oprah, for a lifetime of being committed to the wellbeing of our children and for giving child abuse issues such wonderful coverage on your show. You wrote the original blueprint for this law, and we're grateful, becoming a

tireless advocate for its passage, lobbying Members of Congress of both parties for more than two years, and lobbying the President—people occasionally do that, too. All of us, but especially our children, owe you their gratitude.[55]

Oprah Winfrey's advocacy was so key in winning the passage of the National Child Protection Act in 1993 that it was nicknamed Oprah's Bill. Here she witnesses then-president Bill Clinton signing the act into law.

President Bush, Call Oprah

More recently, in the aftermath of Hurricane Katrina, Winfrey again used her tremendous popularity to inspire political and popular support—not just money. Winfrey went to New Orleans, and millions of people watched her shows about the hurricane's survivors (and those who did not survive). For example, she went into the Superdome, where thousands of people stranded by the storm were living in conditions of filth and disease, and she demanded quick relief.

Many observers contrasted Winfrey's actions with those of the federal government, which was severely criticized for its lack of speed and compassionate response. Writer Paul Harris commented at the time, "As President George W. Bush struggled to cope with the crisis, it was Oprah who set the tone of national shock."[56] And syndicated columnist Maureen Ryan angrily asked, "Can someone tell President Bush to call Oprah?"[57]

In the years to come, Winfrey will no doubt continue to use her power to expand this political and social activism as well as to expand her philanthropy and her personal media empire.

Chapter 6

The Future

Winfrey is still only in her fifties, with years of her career and life still ahead. And *The Oprah Winfrey Show* is still enormously popular. Meanwhile, she recently announced a contract to continue producing the show through 2011. This date will mark the program's twenty-fifth anniversary, at which point Winfrey may retire it.

No one can say with certainty how the show will change or evolve in the years before it ends. One thing that is definitely not in *The Oprah Winfrey Show*'s future, however, is another Emmy Award. In 2000, after the show had already won some thirty-five of television's top honors for excellence, Winfrey permanently took the program out of consideration.

Clearly, though, Winfrey did not plan to rest. She has kept very busy since then. And she has many future projects in the works.

For example, in 2008 she announced plans to create her own television network. Winfrey plans to transform an existing cable network, the Discovery Health Channel, into OWN: the Oprah Winfrey Network, with the potential to reach an estimated 70 million viewers. Due to debut in 2009, the Oprah Winfrey Network, like her magazines and television show, will provide Winfrey's fans with a wide range of programming "designed to entertain, inform and inspire people to live their best lives."[58]

Winfrey also plans to create several reality television shows. These are in various stages of production; the only one that has so far aired, *Oprah's Big Give,* debuted in 2007. On this show, ten

The Oprah Winfrey Show won *so many Emmy Awards that Oprah took the show out of consideration for the award permanently in 2000.*

Oprah Trivia, Part Three

And still more fun facts:

- Three presidents, four first ladies, one reigning queen, one former queen, six princesses, six princes, one earl, one lord, one count, and one duchess have been on *The Oprah Winfrey Show* stage.

- "Dr. Phil" (Phil McGraw) has been a guest on the show more than one hundred times.

- After she accepted her seventh Emmy for Outstanding Talk Show Host and the ninth Emmy for *The Oprah Winfrey Show*, Winfrey took herself and the show out of Emmy consideration. It has won a total of thirty-five Emmy awards in various categories.

- In 1998 Oprah took voice lessons so that she could sing her own theme song, "Run On." She also produced her first and only music video for the song.

- Musical greats such as Paul Simon, Quincy Jones, and Patti LaBelle have written lyrics for *Oprah* theme songs.

Adapted from Oprah.com, "*The Oprah Winfrey Show* Trivia: 20 Years in the Making!" www.oprah.com/presents/2005/20anniv/tows/tows_trivia.jhtml.

people were given large sums of money and resources. They then competed to give these prizes away to strangers in creative and useful ways. The winner of the competition received $1 million—half to keep and half to give away.

The show was a success with audiences, but it only ran for one season. According to some sources, Winfrey was unhappy with the program. She may have been hurt by the poor reaction many critics had to it. These critics acknowledged Winfrey's good intentions, but deplored what they saw as an emphasis on loudly announcing its charity—as opposed to doing good works quietly. They also criticized the show for sometimes giving inappropriate gifts to people, rather than things they really needed. *USA Today* writer Robert Blanco comments about the show, "Altruism [unselfishness] shares space with publicity-masked-as-charity, all wrapped in the familiar reality-genre clichés. And at the stomach-churning center is that old American TV belief that every problem can be solved with a take-home prize, without any consideration for underlying difficulties."[59]

"She Was Meant to Be a Mother"

Another project Winfrey will continue to be intimately involved with in the future is her Leadership Academy in South Africa. The academy has been the subject of ongoing criticism and investigation. Chief among these have been allegations of misconduct, including restrictions on visiting time for the girls with family members and physical abuse on the part of one school employee.

Oprah hugs a student at the Oprah Winfrey Leadership Academy for Girls in South Africa.

Despite these problems (which were apparently worked out), Winfrey remains deeply committed to the academy. It is scheduled to reach full capacity of 450 girls by 2011. Winfrey's future plans include teaching leadership classes there via satellite and spending much of her retirement in a house she is building on campus.

Winfrey's commitment to the young women of her academy is very strong. It is so strong, in fact, that she has stated her belief that the reason she never had children was because the academy girls were meant to be her daughters. Winfrey's friend Gayle King comments, "When I watched Oprah with those girls, I kept thinking she was meant to be a mother, and it would happen one way or another."[60]

Political Action

Another big part of the future for Winfrey will be her increasing political outspokenness and influence. In recent years she has not hesitated to rally her fans toward causes she believes in.

Oprah Winfrey was a vocal supporter of President Barack Obama's political campaign.

For instance, she has been vocal in her criticisms of war in the Middle East. In 2003, as President George W. Bush was gearing up to invade Iraq, Winfrey produced a show that included clips of people from all over the world asking America not to go to war. Not all of America's television stations were pleased, and some chose not to run the show. In several parts of the East Coast, it was replaced by network broadcasts of a press conference in which Bush and Secretary of State Colin Powell summarized their case for war.

Winfrey was critical of Bush's policies on several other occasions. For instance, in 2006 she aired a show entitled "Is War the Only Answer?" Part of an ongoing series exploring tensions in the Middle East, it proved to be quite controversial. In fact, Winfrey commented that the show generated more hate mail than she had ever received.

More recently, the television host was a high-profile supporter of Barack Obama's 2008 presidential campaign. (They are long-time friends and attended the same church in Chicago.) Winfrey held a number of important fund-raisers and appeared at rallies to promote the Illinois senator. Many observers saw her endorsement as an important boost in Obama's success.

However, Winfrey says that she is not interested in personally entering politics. A number of people have, sometimes half-jokingly, suggested that she would make a great politician—even president. But Winfrey feels that she can make a greater difference by being on television, presenting issues and trying to bring about positive change. She states, "I think I could have a great influence in politics, and I think I could get elected. . . . But I think that what I do every day has far more impact."[61]

Spirituality

Another aspect of Winfrey's life and career that will figure large in her future revolves around her interest in spirituality and personal growth. Over the years Winfrey has moved away from (or added to) the deep Christian faith she grew up with. In her own life, she has combined the lessons and beliefs of Christianity with those of many other schools of thought.

Writer Deepak Chopra is one of several spiritually oriented guests Oprah Winfrey has had on her show.

When Winfrey began to emphasize this spirituality and personal growth on her show, she made a serious commitment for the future. She announced that, from then on, *The Oprah Winfrey Show* would be dedicated to making the world a better place—and to helping her viewers be better people. She stated, "I want you to know that . . . I am going to continue to try to strive to be a light in the world and to offer self-enlightenment to those who choose to watch."[62]

The result has been her support of a number of techniques, philosophies, and belief systems. She frequently has guests who advocate these methods. One regular on her show, for instance, is Marianne Williamson, an activist and author whose books about spirituality include *A Return to Love*. Other regular guests who emphasize spirituality and personal growth include such writer-speakers as Deepak Chopra, Eckhart Tolle, and Dr. Wayne Dyer.

"The Church of O"

Winfrey's emphasis on spirituality has been enormously popular, eagerly embraced by millions of her fans. Indeed, to many observers, Winfrey is on her way to becoming one of the world's most significant spiritual guides. Religion writer LaTonya Taylor, in an article titled "The Church of O," reflects on this phenomenon:

> Since 1994, when she abandoned traditional talk-show fare for more edifying content . . . Oprah's most significant role has become that of spiritual leader. To her audience . . . she has become a postmodern priestess—an icon of church-free spirituality. . . . Much like a healthy church, Oprah creates community, provides information, and encourages people to evaluate and improve their lives.[63]

But Winfrey has also come under considerable criticism for pursuing and advocating her spiritual path in such a public way. One example of this criticism concerns the flap over a controversial self-help program called "The Secret." According to The Secret's agenda, people can change their lives with positive thoughts, causing vibrations that result in good things happening to them. Winfrey began featuring segments about this system in 2007.

Criticism

Its critics argue that the ideas behind The Secret, despite having been in circulation for many years, are unproven pseudoscience. These critics are concerned that following such an unproven course of action might be psychologically damaging to some people. And they worry that The Secret promotes little more than selfish materialism and superficial responses to important decisions.

Furthermore, they argue that Winfrey's very public promotion of it is irresponsible, given her vast influence. Writing on Salon.com, Peter Birkenhead comments on this, referring to the earlier scandal when James Frey's memoir, chosen for Oprah's Book Club, was found to be largely invented. He writes, "If James Frey deserved to be raked over the coals [by Winfrey] for lying about how drunk he was, doesn't Oprah deserve some scrutiny for pitching the meretricious [plausible but insincere] nonsense in 'The Secret'?"[64]

Despite such criticism, however, Winfrey has defended her decision to publicly discuss The Secret and the many other spiritual subjects that interest her. But, she cautions, people should think for themselves, and they should avoid simply tagging along with whatever she does. "Don't follow in *my* footsteps," she says. "Initiate your own guidance. Often intuition will direct you. If it feels right, it probably is right."[65]

Health Gossip

Still another aspect of Winfrey's life and career that will figure in her future is the issue of gossip. Ever since she first gained fame, Winfrey has been the target of virtually nonstop speculation about her personal life. Her fans' appetite for knowing everything they can about their idol seems to be insatiable.

There are many recurring themes for the gossip that circulates about Winfrey. One of the best-known topics is her ever-present weight problem, which is connected (as it is with all people) to her overall well-being.

Generally, Winfrey has worked hard to make sure her health has been excellent, and it often pays off. For instance, in 1995, to celebrate her fortieth birthday, she ran a marathon in Washington, D.C. (She finished in a respectable four hours, twenty-nine minutes, and fifteen seconds.) Recently, she has also promoted (and taken part in) a vegetarian diet and a "21-Day Cleanse" program designed to rid the body of unhealthy toxins.

However, sometimes her health has given her problems. For instance, it appears that one of Winfrey's health concerns may be

Oprah Winfrey and Mad Cows

Winfrey has been the target of controversy since she first began, and no doubt she will continue to draw criticism in the future. Often, controversy arises from subjects that are discussed on her show.

For instance, in 1996, as part of a program on dangerous food, she aired a segment about mad cow disease, a dangerous disease that can be carried by tainted beef. On air, Winfrey commented that the information she was learning "has just stopped me cold from eating another burger."

This infuriated a group of Texas cattlemen. They sued Winfrey, claiming that her comment sent beef prices plummeting and had cost the industry $12 million. After a trial in Texas (during which she broadcast daily from a temporary studio), she was found not liable.

Quoted in BBC World News, "Oprah Winfrey Faces Mad Cow Libel Suit," January 20, 1998. http://news.bbc.co.uk/1/hi/world/48964.stm.

a factor in her fluctuating weight. In October 2007 the television host revealed that she had been diagnosed with a thyroid disorder. (The thyroid is a gland in the neck that controls how quickly the body burns energy and makes proteins.) The disorder has apparently been responsible for Winfrey's periodic bouts of exhaustion and weakness, and there is some evidence that it is connected with her weight fluctuation as well.

Personal Life Gossip

Of course, other aspects of Winfrey's private life are also fuel for gossip and speculation. For instance, there is the question of her ongoing romance with Stedman Graham. The two frequently tell reporters that they have a "spiritual" relationship, but Winfrey's

In addition to running a marathon on her fortieth birthday, Oprah Winfrey has participated in several runs for charity, such as this 5 km race to benefit women's cancer organizations in 1997.

fans want to know—will they ever marry?

Then there was the question of Winfrey's problematic family. Her half brother, Jeffrey, whose existence she had not publicly admitted for years, was a gay drug user who died of AIDS. And her half sister, Patricia, also had a drug problem. Patricia was unable to care for her two children, despite going through rehab. For years, Winfrey did what she could for her sister and nieces.

Then, in 1992, Patricia revealed the story of Winfrey's teenage pregnancy to a tabloid newspaper in exchange for nineteen thousand dollars. Winfrey later admitted the truth of the story, but she was devastated and furious. She did not speak with her sister for two years. Patricia died in 2003, apparently from a drug overdose.

Even unfounded rumors about Winfrey are routinely given a great deal of attention in the tabloid press. One recurring rumor, for example, concerns Winfrey's relationship with Gayle King, now an editor at *O, The Oprah Magazine.*

The rumors allege that the two are gay. King and Winfrey have been best friends since their early twenties, and Winfrey says that the rumors exist only because of their unusually long and close relationship. She states,

> I understand why people think we're gay. There isn't a definition in our culture for this kind of bond between women. So I get why people have to label it—how can you

be this close without it being sexual? . . . I've told nearly everything there is to tell [about myself]. All my stuff is out there. People think I'd be so ashamed of being gay that I wouldn't admit it? Oh, please.[66]

"A Lot of Fun"

Rumors, speculation, and intense curiosity about one's private life are perhaps inevitable for people as famous and visible as Winfrey. Typically, intrusion into their private lives tends to make celebrities resentful, and Winfrey is no exception. Nonetheless, life in a fishbowl, being constantly under scrutiny, does not seem to have made her miserable.

In fact, she says, being Oprah is, overall, pretty great. She comments, "It's a lot of fun. I can tell you that. It really is a *lot* of fun. It certainly is more *fun* than I thought it was going to be."[67]

Winfrey and Hermès

Sometimes controversy swirls around Winfrey's private life. For example, in 2005 she made international news after being denied access to the plush flagship boutique of the Hermès company in Paris, France. She had arrived fifteen minutes after closing time and could see activity inside. Hermès often extends hours for celebrity customers, but that evening the shop was preparing for a private event and asked her to come back the next day.

There were some indications that Winfrey believed that a white celebrity would have been allowed in. This may or may not have been the case. In any event, she was furious and, despite a public apology from the company, called for a boycott of Hermès products. This boycott was lifted after the head of Hermès USA came on her show to apologize for his employee's rudeness.

Oprah Winfrey enjoys her life and her accomplishments. Her opportunity to make a difference in the world has also brought her fulfillment.

And, it seems, it is also fulfilling. Being Oprah has given Winfrey an astonishing chance to make a difference in the world and to leave something very real for the future. This opportunity has already been proven by her ability to influence social programs and movements, her desire to help and inspire individuals, and her unselfish willingness to donate much of her fortune to charity.

The opportunity to make a difference will continue in the years to come. About the future, Winfrey says, "I want to be working on projects that are meaningful. I know that can sound superficial. But it's true. I would like to be able to say, down the road, that I created a legacy, something even more enduring than anything I've done yet."[68] If Winfrey's millions of fans have anything to say about it, she will continue to do just that.

Notes

Introduction: It's Oprah!

1. Marcia Z. Nelson, *The Gospel According to Oprah.* Louisville, KY: Westminster John Knox, 2005, p. vii.
2. Quoted in Nelson, *The Gospel According to Oprah,* p. xix.
3. Paul Harris, "You Go, Girl: The Observer Profile," *Guardian*, November 20, 2005, p. 27. http://observer.guardian.co.uk/comment/story/0,6903,1646654,00.html?gusrc=rss.
4. Quoted in *Time*, "TIME 100: The World's Most Influential People," June 8, 1998. www.time.com/time/time100/artists/profile/winfrey.html.
5. Quoted in Bill Adler, *The Uncommon Wisdom of Oprah Winfrey.* Secaucus, NJ: Birch Lane, 1997, p. 42.
6. Quoted in Adler, *The Uncommon Wisdom of Oprah Winfrey*, p. 167.

Chapter 1: Starting Out

7. Harris, "You Go, Girl," p. 27.
8. Quoted in Adler, *The Uncommon Wisdom of Oprah Winfrey*, p. 3.
9. Quoted in Adler, *The Uncommon Wisdom of Oprah Winfrey*, p. 4.
10. Quoted in George Mair, *Oprah Winfrey: The Real Story.* New York: Birch Lane, 1994, p. 8.
11. Quoted in LaTonya Taylor, "The Church of O," *Christianity Today*, April 1, 2002. www.christianitytoday.com/ct/article_print.html?id=8491.
12. Quoted in Mair, *Oprah Winfrey*, p. 14.
13. Quoted in Adler, *The Uncommon Wisdom of Oprah Winfrey*, p. 8.
14. Quoted in Aldore D. Collier, "Oprah Honors Her Heroes at Three-Day Bash in Santa Barbara, CA," *Jet*, June 6, 2005. http://findarticles.com/p/articles/mi_m1355/is_23_107/ai_n13810449.

15. Quoted in Adler, *The Uncommon Wisdom of Oprah Winfrey*, p. 261.
16. Quoted in Mair, *Oprah Winfrey*, p. 17.
17. Quoted in Mair, *Oprah Winfrey*, p. 19.
18. Quoted in Adler, *The Uncommon Wisdom of Oprah Winfrey*, p. 127.
19. Quoted in Taylor, "The Church of O."
20. Quoted in Adler, *The Uncommon Wisdom of Oprah Winfrey*, p. 86.
21. Quoted in Adler, *The Uncommon Wisdom of Oprah Winfrey*, p. 229.

Chapter 2: On Television

22. Quoted in Mair, *Oprah Winfrey*, p. 36.
23. Quoted in Richard Zoglin, "Lady with a Calling," *Time*, August 8, 1988. www.time.com/time/magazine/article/0,9171, 968069,00.html.
24. Quoted in Mair, *Oprah Winfrey*, pp. 44–45.
25. Quoted in Zoglin, "Lady with a Calling."
26. Quoted in Adler, *The Uncommon Wisdom of Oprah Winfrey*, p. 48.
27. Quoted in Turner Classic Movies, *The Color Purple*. www .tcm.com/thismonth/article/?cid=76270&rss=mrqe.
28. Quoted in Adler, *The Uncommon Wisdom of Oprah Winfrey*, p. 197.

Chapter 3: *Oprah* Evolves

29. Quoted in Janice Peck, *The Age of Oprah*. Boulder, CO: Paradigm, 2008, p. 2.
30. Zoglin, "Lady with a Calling."
31. Cecilia Konchar Farr, *Reading Oprah: How Oprah's Book Club Changed the Way America Reads*. Albany: State University of New York Press, 2005, p. 9.
32. Quoted in Adler, *The Uncommon Wisdom of Oprah Winfrey*, p. 57.
33. Quoted in Mair, *Oprah Winfrey*, p. 268.
34. Quoted in Nelson, *The Gospel According to Oprah*, p. 59.
35. Quoted in Alessandra Stanley, "Tom Cruise on 'Oprah,' With-

out Gymnastics," *New York Times*, May 3, 2008. www.ny times.com/2008/05/03/arts/television/03watc.html?fta=y.

36. Quoted in Oprah.com, "Our Most Forgettable Shows." www2.oprah.com/tows/pastshows/tows_1999/tows_past_199 90226.jhtml.

37. Quoted in Adler, *The Uncommon Wisdom of Oprah Winfrey*, p. 17.

38. Nelson, *The Gospel According to Oprah*, p. xiv.

Chapter 4: Expanding the Oprah Empire

39. Quoted in Adler, *The Uncommon Wisdom of Oprah Winfrey*, p. 146.

40. Quoted in Adler, *The Uncommon Wisdom of Oprah Winfrey*, p. 134.

41. Mark Steyn, "Comic Oprah," *National Review*, March 23, 1998. www.nationalreview.com/23mar98/steyn032398.html.

42. Quoted in Dana Kennedy, "Oprah Act Two," *Entertainment Weekly*, September 9, 1994. www.ew.com/ew/article/0,,3035 83,00.html.

43. Quoted in Farr, *Reading Oprah*, p. 26.

44. Farr, *Reading Oprah*, p. 1.

45. Harris, "You Go, Girl," p. 27.

46. Quoted in Peck, *The Age of Oprah*, p. 175.

Chapter 5: Giving It Away

47. Quoted in Stephen M. Silverman with Susan Mandel, "Oprah Winfrey: Wealth Is 'a Good Thing,'" *People*, April 11, 2006. www.people.com/people/article/0,,1182572,00.html.

48. Quoted in Zoglin, "Lady with a Calling."

49. Quoted in Mark Thornton, "Oprah's Father Attends Ceremony to Kick Off Construction on Boys & Girls Club," *Kosciusko (MS) Star-Herald*, October 6, 2004. www.bgcattala. org/main_sublinks.asp?id=1&sid=51.

50. Quoted in Peck, *The Age of Oprah*, p. 219.

51. Quoted in Allison Samuels, "Oprah Goes to School," *Newsweek*, January 8, 2007. www.newsweek.com/id/56724/ output/print.

52. Quoted in Samuels, "Oprah Goes to School."

53. Quoted in Collier, "Oprah Honors Her Heroes at Three-Day Bash in Santa Barbara, CA."
54. Quoted in Collier, "Oprah Honors Her Heroes at Three-Day Bash in Santa Barbara, CA."
55. Bill Clinton, "Remarks on Signing the National Child Protection Act of 1993," BNet. http://findarticles.com/p/articles/mi_m2889/is_n51_v29/ai_15155522.
56. Harris, "You Go, Girl," p. 27.
57. Quoted in Harris, "You Go, Girl," p. 27.

Chapter 6: The Future

58. Oprah.com, "Oprah Winfrey and Discovery Communications to Form New Joint Venture: OWN: The Oprah Winfrey Network." www.oprah.com/about/events/about_events_announcement.jhtml.
59. Robert Blanco, "'Oprah's Big Give' Puts Good Works in a Bad Light," *USA Today*, March 2, 2008. www.usatoday.com/life/television/reviews/2008-02-28-oprahs-big-give_N.htm.
60. Quoted in Samuels, "Oprah Goes to School."
61. Quoted in Peck, *The Age of Oprah*, pp. 2–3.
62. Quoted in Peck, *The Age of Oprah*, p. 128.
63. Taylor, "The Church of O."
64. Peter Birkenhead, "Oprah's Ugly Secret," Salon.com, March 5, 2007. www.salon.com/mwt/feature/2007/03/05/the_secret.
65. Quoted in Adler, *The Uncommon Wisdom of Oprah Winfrey*, p. 227.
66. Quoted in Marla Lehner, "Oprah: Gayle and I Are Not Gay," *People*, July 18, 2006. www.people.com/people/article/0,26334,1215402,00.html.
67. Quoted in Adler, *The Uncommon Wisdom of Oprah Winfrey*, p. 115.
68. Quoted in Adler, *The Uncommon Wisdom of Oprah Winfrey*, p. 97.

1954

On January 29 Orpah Gail Winfrey is born in Kosciusko, a small town in central Mississippi. Her name later becomes *Oprah*, perhaps due to a mistake on the birth certificate.

1958

Oprah's mother, Vernita Lee, moves Oprah to Milwaukee, Wisconsin.

1962

Oprah goes to live for a year in Nashville, Tennessee, with her father, Vernon Winfrey, and his wife, Zelma. She is much happier there than in Milwaukee.

1968

After several years back in Milwaukee, rebellious Oprah is nearly committed to a home for wayward girls. Instead, she returns to Nashville. She thrives there and excels in school.

1970–1971

While still in high school, Winfrey lands her first job: reading the news on radio station WVOL. She continues there part time after graduating from high school and enrolling at Tennessee State University on a full scholarship.

1974

Winfrey leaves college to become the first African American, and the youngest person ever, to be a television news anchor in Nashville at WLAC (now WTVF).

1976

She moves to a much bigger city, Baltimore, Maryland, to join WJZ-TV. In 1978 she begins cohosting a daily talk show that is extremely popular.

1984

Winfrey becomes a talk-show host on WLS in Chicago, Illinois, one of the nation's top television markets. The show is an instant hit.

1985

The Color Purple, a film by Steven Spielberg, is released. In her first serious acting job, Winfrey has a supporting role and is later nominated for an Academy Award. She attends the ceremony with Stedman Graham, who would soon become her life partner.

1986

The Oprah Winfrey Show goes national. At thirty-two, Winfrey becomes a millionaire and the first African American television host to be nationally syndicated. Two years later, she becomes the first black person (and one of the first women) to head a major movie/television studio. It houses her production company, Harpo.

1989

Winfrey's show changes direction, leaving behind sensationalistic themes in favor of topics meant to help her viewers have better, more spiritually fulfilling lives.

Late 1980s–Present

Winfrey is involved in numerous film and television projects, including *Beloved* and *Their Eyes Were Watching God*. She expands her empire in other ways as well, including a popular Web site, magazines, books, a cable television network, and a Broadway musical version of *The Color Purple*.

Early 1990s–Present

Winfrey actively gives away hundreds of millions of dollars. By now the richest self-made woman in America and the first black woman billionaire in history, she is ranked in 2006 as thirty-second on *BusinessWeek* magazine's annual list of the nation's fifty most generous philanthropists. She also becomes increasingly active in politics, including playing a major role in the 1993 passage of the so-called Oprah's Law to mandate a national data bank of convicted child abusers.

2008

Winfrey announces that her show will run at least through 2011, marking the program's twenty-fifth anniversary.

For More Information

Books

Bill Adler, *The Uncommon Wisdom of Oprah Winfrey*. Secaucus, NJ: Birch Lane, 1997. This unauthorized "biography" is actually a collection of Winfrey quotations drawn from interviews.

Ilene Cooper, *Oprah Winfrey, Media Queen*. New York: Viking, 2007. Part of the Up Close series.

Katherine Krohn, *Oprah Winfrey*. Minneapolis: Lerner, 2002. Part of the Biography series connected to the A&E television series of the same name.

Sherry Beck Paprocki, *Oprah Winfrey: Talk Show Host and Media Magnate*. New York: Chelsea House, 2006. This is a nicely written biography in a series called Black Americans of Achievement.

Robin Westen, *Oprah Winfrey: "I Don't Believe in Failure."* Berkley Heights, NJ: Enslow, 2005. Part of the series The African-American Biography Library, this is a good short biography for young adults.

Oprah Winfrey, *Journey to Beloved*. New York: Hyperion, 1998. This is a chronicle of the making of the film *Beloved*, with journal excerpts, essays, and beautiful photos.

Periodicals

Bill Clinton, "Remarks on Signing the National Child Protection Act of 1993," BNet. http://findarticles.com/p/articles/mi_m28 89/is_n51_v29/ai_15155522. A transcript of the president's comments about "the Oprah Bill."

Paul Harris, "You Go, Girl: The Observer Profile," *Guardian*, November 20, 2005. http://observer.guardian.co.uk/comment/story/0,6903,1646654,00.html?gusrc=rss. A good, in-depth profile.

Dana Kennedy, "Oprah Act Two," *Entertainment Weekly*, September 9, 1994. www.ew.com/ew/article/0,,303583,00.html. A piece on Winfrey's changing show.

Allison Samuels, "Oprah Goes to School," *Newsweek*, January 8, 2007. www.newsweek.com/id/56724/output/print. This article focuses on Winfrey's South African Leadership Academy.

Stephen M. Silverman with Susan Mandel, "Oprah Winfrey: Wealth Is 'a Good Thing,'" *People*, April 11, 2006. www.people.com/people/article/0,,1182572,00.html. An article in which Winfrey talks about being rich.

Alessandra Stanley, "Tom Cruise on 'Oprah,' Without Gymnastics," *New York Times*, May 3, 2008. www.nytimes.com/2008/05/03/arts/television/03watc.html?fta=y. A newspaper piece about Cruise's interview with Winfrey following his infamous "jumping" interview.

Richard Zoglin, "Lady with a Calling," *Time*, August 8, 1988. www.time.com/time/magazine/article/0,9171,968069,00.html. A profile from the beginning of Winfrey's rise to fame.

DVDs

African American Lives. DVD. Arlington, VA: PBS Home Video, 2006. This is the series in which the ancestry of several prominent people, including Winfrey, is traced back to reveal many generations in their families.

Beloved. DVD. Directed by Jonathan Demme. Burbank, CA: Touchstone Home Video, 1998. In this film of Toni Morrison's novel, Winfrey stars as Sethe, an ex-slave.

The Color Purple. DVD. Directed by Steven Spielberg. Burbank, CA: Warner Home Video, 2003. This is the film version of Walker's novel that earned Winfrey a supporting-actress Oscar nomination.

Henry Louis Gates Jr., *Finding Oprah's Roots: Finding Your Own*. DVD. Arlington, VA: PBS Home Video, 2006. Historian Gates uses his own family and that of Winfrey to lead viewers through the process of finding out more about their own family histories.

The Oprah Winfrey Show: 20th Anniversary Collection. DVD. Hollywood, CA: Paramount Home Entertainment, 2005. This presents highlights of Winfrey's first twenty years as host of her own show.

Web Sites

Oprah.com (www.oprah.com). The extensive official site of Oprah Winfrey.

Oprah's Angel Network (http://oprahsangelnetwork.org). The official site of Winfrey's charity organization.

Oprah Winfrey: People.com (www.people.com/people/oprah_winfrey). The popular celebrity-gossip magazine's site devoted to Winfrey.

YouTube—Oprah's Channel (www.youtube.com/oprah). Winfrey's channel on YouTube, with numerous clips.

Adam Woog has written many books for adults, young adults, and children. He lives in Seattle, Washington, with his wife and their daughter.

Woog has had only one television talk-show experience, which happened while he was promoting a book. He was double-billed with a water-skiing squirrel.